T0370049

SUBMARINES OF WORLD WAR II

SUBMARINES
OF WORLD WAR II
1939–45

E.V. MARTINDALE

amber
BOOKS

First published in 2024

Copyright © 2024 Amber Books Ltd

All rights reserved. No part of this publication may be reproduced,
stored in a retrieval system, or transmitted in any form or by any
means, electronic, mechanical, photocopying, recording, or otherwise,
without prior written permission of the copyright holder.

Amber Books Ltd
United House
North Road
London N7 9DP
United Kingdom
www.amberbooks.co.uk
Facebook: amberbooks
YouTube: amberbooksltd
Instagram: amberbooksltd
X(Twitter): @amberbooks

ISBN: 978-1-83886-463-7

Editor: Michael Spilling
Design: Andrew Easton
Picture research: Terry Forshaw

Printed in China

Contents

Introduction

Of all warship types in action between 1939 and 1945, the submarine was the one that underwent the greatest degree of change and development. Surface ships were of course subject to improvement and updating, but these were established ship types that changed little in essentials throughout the war, though with many new kinds of ancillary equipment. Only aircraft carriers (the submarine's nemesis) could rival submarines in the extent of development as a warship type in the war years.

In the interwar decades, much of the work done on submarine design was experimental, trying out different types (though the British even proposed in 1921 and 1930 that naval submarines should be banned). This reflected some uncertainty about the way in which submarines might be used in the event of a war, and navies explored various answers depending on their own geographical position and strategic plans. Coastal and inshore defence? Commerce raiding in the oceans? Fleet support as scouts? A wide variety of types ensued. Italy and Japan were the

most consistent in maintaining design programmes – at least until 1937–38. But there were few innovations.

In September 1939, the world's navies possessed around 770 submarines, many of them obsolete and most of them obsolescent. In the early years of the war, new boats were built in a hurry based on pre-war designs. However, progress in other industries, such as metallurgy, construction methods, engine design and electronics, was now applied to submarine design and construction, and a succession of new classes

The crew of U-47 taking the salute from the crew of the German battleship *Scharnhorst* on its return from the successful attack at Scapa Flow in October 1939.

and sub-classes was built by the major navies, especially the German *Kriegsmarine*.

During 1939–45, parallel advances were made in methods of detecting, identifying and destroying submarines. There were some cases in which one submarine was sunk by another (though only one with both submerged: see British V-class). But the toll taken by surface vessels and aircraft was huge. Increasing Allied control of the sea and air made existence ever

more perilous for German and Japanese submarines and their crews at a time when most submarines could not go much deeper than 100m (330ft).

Had the submarine outlived its usefulness as a weapon? Or could a new generation of submarine types change the situation? It was the Germans and Japanese who most felt the need to face this challenge but with results too late to influence the outcome in 1945.

In June 1941, the British submarines stationed at Lazzaretto Creek, Malta, were grouped as the 10th Submarine Flotilla, and the Lazzaretto itself was named HMS *Talbot*. The nearest submarine is HMS *Upholder*.

PART 1: THE AXIS POWERS

The German U-boat designs of 1917–18 formed the basis of new submarine projects for both Germany and Japan in the 1920s (Japan received nine U-boats to study). National strategy ensured different lines of development. Clandestine action was taken by Germany to evade the terms of the Treaty of Versailles with the assistance of Dutch constructors and the Finnish Navy. The focus was on designing relatively small craft for coastal defence.

For Japan, the aim was to counter the expansion of American influence in the Pacific region, and this required large submarines capable of long-range cruising and ocean reconnaissance. Only with the advent of the Nazi regime in 1933 did Germany have a publicly acknowledged submarine building programme. From September 1939, Germany in particular began a massive increase of its small U-boat fleet.

Type VII U-boats at Wilhelmshaven, apparently after the surrender of 4 May 1945. The deck guns were removed before the end of the war.

Italy followed up its own World War I building programme with a range of types, including long-range patrol craft, to defend its colonial possessions in East and North Africa and minelayers. The Regia Marina had one of the largest submarine forces in 1939, relatively up to date in design, with numerous classes which exhibited fairly small differences. Entering World War II in December 1941, Japan included submarines in the surprise attack on Pearl Harbor, but they played a negligible part. For national strategic reasons, Japanese submarines were mostly large, and of its 48 submarines in service at that time, 41 carried one or more aircraft.

The following types feature in this chapter:

GERMANY
- Type IA
- Type II
- Type VII
- Type IX
- Type XIV
- Type XB
- Type XXI
- Type XXIII

JAPAN
- Type C-1
- Type B-1
- Type KD7
- Type KS Ro 100
- Type I-400
- Type I-201
- Sh (Sen-Ho) Type 1-351
- Type Ha 201

ITALY
- Pisani and Mameli classes
- Balilla and Calvi classes
- Squalo and Sirena classes
- Adua class
- Foca and Marcello classes
- Marconi and Cagni classes
- CB-class midget submarine
- U-class
- Flutto class

I-171, a *Kaidai*-class cruiser submarine of the KD6 sub-class, looking forward from the quarterdeck, in April 1939.

Type IA (1936–40)

The two Type IA boats paved the way for the *Kriegsmarine's* wartime ocean-going flotillas, particularly the Type IX.

German designers working with the Dutch bureau *Ingenieurskantoor voor Scheepsbouw* were on the project from the mid-1920s. Semi-secret work also went on in Spain and Finland. A Spanish yard, *Echevarietta* in Cadiz, built a single prototype, known as E-1, launched in October 1930 (later sold to Turkey).

Construction of Type IA began only in 1934 at the Deschimag A.G. Weser yard in Bremen. The design was double-hulled, with the outer hull drawn down to keel level. Ballast tanks and fuel bunkers were placed between the hulls. These were among the earliest submarines to have electrically welded hulls, though the rolled carbon steel used in construction limited diving range to 100m (330ft). A serrated cable cutter was permanently mounted on the bow, as was typical on most submarines in the early war years.

The tower was of basic bathtub shape, which would remain typical of U-boats up to Type XXI with a narrower extension aft. A 105mm (4.1in) gun was placed forward of the tower, and a 20mm (0.79in) AA gun was mounted at bridge level on the after part. Four bow and two stern 533mm (21in) torpedo tubes were fitted, with either G7e (electric drive) or G7v (compressed air) torpedoes depending on availability. Fourteen torpedoes could be carried. The boats could also be used for minelaying, with reduced torpedo capacity.

Limitations

Their defects, as much as their qualities, showed the way forward. Surface balance was poor, with rolling and pitching. Rudder and propeller arrangement restricted manoeuvrability. The MAN M 8 V 40/46 eight-cylinder diesel engines were not reliable. These developed a maximum 1148kW (1540hp). The two double Brown Boveri electric motors were rated at 373kW (500hp). Two AFA 36 MAK 40 62-cell battery sets were fitted, with a weight of 97.5 tonnes (96t). The operating range of 6700nm (12,395km, 7712mi) was modest for an ocean-going boat.

No further Type IAs were built, and IB remained on the drawing board. U-25 and U-26 proved useful as training vessels, but in 1939 they could scarcely be regarded as fit for battle. However, both saw active service and sank several merchant ships and small warships before being lost in minefields in 1940.

U-25 (Type IA)

Dimensions: Length 72.39m (237.5ft), Beam 6.21m (20.4ft), Draught 4.3m (14.1ft)
Displacement (surface/submerged): 875.8 tonnes (862t) / 998.7 tonnes (983t)
Propulsion: two 1044kW (1400hp) diesels; two double 373kW (500hp) electric motors, two screws
Speed (surface/submerged): 17.75kt (32.8kmh, 20.4mph) / 8.3kt (15.35kmh, 9.54mph)
Range (surface/submerged): 6700nm (12,395km, 7712mi) at 12kt / 78nm (144km, 90mi) at 4kt
Armament: six 533mm (21in) torpedo tubes, 14 torpedoes. One 105mm (4.1in) SKC/36 gun; one 20mm (0.79in) Flak/30 AA gun
Crew: 43

U-25 (Type IA)

U-25 could carry 14 torpedoes or four torpedoes, plus mines of both TMA and TMB type, or a maximum of 28 TMA or 42 TMB, with no torpedoes.

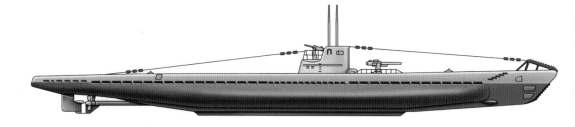

Type II (1935–41)

Fifty boats in four variations from IIA to IID were produced. Its design history goes back to the UF class of World War I, via the one-off Finnish-built prototype *Vesikko* (1933).

The type leader was U-1, launched at Deutsche Werk, Kiel in 1935. It had a small tower, with narrow bridge space, and a single fixed-eyepiece periscope.

The main differences in the various sub-types were increases in length and displacement, primarily to allow for greater fuel capacity and operating range. But the Type II remained a compact craft, nicknamed *Einbaum* (dugout) by crews, designed for coastal operations. Single-hulled, of welded construction, it was primarily intended as a training type, but the outbreak of war in September 1939 brought many into real action. Later, its small size and vulnerability to attack relegated it once again to training.

With only three torpedo tubes (all forward) and capacity to hold five torpedoes (six on IIC) or 18 mines, and an original range of only 1050nm (1945km, 1208mi), it was intended for short patrols. For the 25-man crew, accommodation was extremely tight: 15 bunks were provided, plus the skipper's cubicle. Propulsion in all Type IIs was by two MWM (Motoren Werke

Mannheim) RS127S six-cylinder marine diesels. The electric motors, two SSW (Siemens-Schukert Werke) GVV322/36, double acting, were uprated to 153kW (205hp) in IIC and IID. The 62-cell battery sets were of either AFA 36/MAK/580 type or the more powerful AFA 44/MAL/570, fitted to some IIB and IIC boats, enabling a maximum submerged endurance of 83nm (154km, 96mi) and 81nm (150km, 93mi) respectively, at 2kt. Oil fuel capacity, 11.8 tonnes (11.61t) in Type IIA, was 23 tonnes (22.7t) in IIC and IID.

The original armament of a twin 20mm (0.79in) AA gun was supplemented in wartime refits, mounted on aftwards railed platforms of the *Wintergarten* type.

Type IIB

The Type IIB was lengthened midships by three frames. Additional internal fuel tanks extended its range to 1800nm (1945km, 1208mi) at 12kt (22.2kmh, 13.8mph). Diving time was reduced to 25–30 seconds. Six IIB boats were dismantled and transported overland

---

U-2 (Type IIA)

Dimensions (length/beam/draught): 40.9m (134.2ft) / 4.1m (13.4ft) / 3.8m (12.5ft)
Displacement (surface/submerged): 254 tonnes (250t) / 303 tonnes (298t)
Propulsion: two MWM 6-cyl 261kW (350hp) diesels; two SSW 134kW (180hp) electric motors, two screws
Speed (surface/submerged): 13kt (24kmh, 14.9mph) / 7.4kt (13.7kmh, 8.5mph)
Range (surface/submerged): 2000nm (3704km, 2302mi) at 8kt / 35nm (64.8km, 40.3mi) at 4kt
Armament: three 533mm (21in) torpedo tubes, six torpedoes; one 20mm (0.79in) Flak twin AA gun
Crew: 25

U-2 (Type IIA)

Though not a large boat, U-2 was built in a very short time: laid down in February 1935 and commissioned on 25 July of the same year, at the Deutsche Werke, Kiel. Its entire career was spent as a training boat, under 10 successive commanders. It sank on 8 April 1944 after colliding with a trawler.

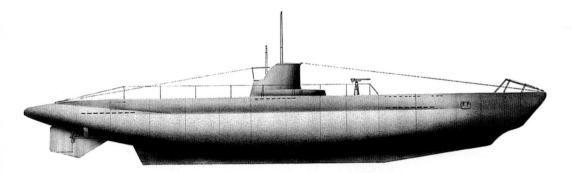

Type IIA training boats U-6 (centre) and U-4 (right) are shown in the docks at Kiel, 1937. Both submarines served with the *UBootschulflottille* until being transferred to the 21st Training Flotilla in July 1940. U-4 made four patrols, sinking three ships and the British submarine HMS *Thistle*. U-6 made two patrols, but had no success.

Type IIB

Known as 'dugouts' to their crews, the Type II coastal boats carried too few torpedoes to be really effective in combat, and most became training vessels.

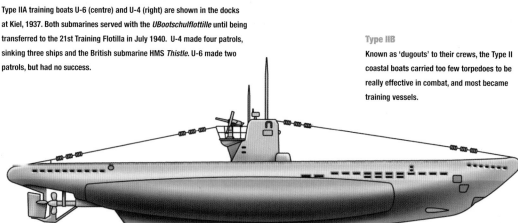

The hatch is open on this Type IIC conning tower. The periscope housing can be seen immediately behind the open hatch. The commander would have stood at the front-right of the tower, next to the voice tube.

from Kiel to the Black Sea in 1942–43. These were armed with a 20mm (0.79in) Flak twin and a 20mm (0.79in) Flak single AA mounting.

The Type IIC was further lengthened by two frames to 43.9m (144ft) to allow for a radio room and a second periscope (removed in U-57 and U-58 to make room for a snorkel pipe in 1943). Its range was extended to 1900nm (3519km, 2186mi).

The Type IID had blister tanks fitted to the hull to increase fuel capacity, increasing the beam to 5m (14.4ft) and giving an increase in range to 3200nm (5926km, 3682mi) at 12.7kt. 'Kort nozzle' ducted propellers were fitted, for quieter running (the British had also experimented with ducted propellers but neither navy made general use of them).

U-137 (Type IID)

Dimensions: Length 44m (144.4ft), Beam 5m (16.4ft), Draught 3.9m (12.8ft)

Displacement (surface/submerged): 319.1 tonnes (314t) / 370 tonnes (364t)

Propulsion: two MWM 6-cyl 261kW (350hp) diesels; two SSW 153kW (205hp) electric motors, two screws

Speed (surface/submerged): 12.7kt (25.5kmh, 14.6mph) / 7.4kt (13.7kmh, 8.5mph)

Range (surface/submerged): 3200nm (5926km, 3683mi) / 56nm (104km, 64.5mi) at 4kt

Armament: three 533mm (21in) torpedo tubes; one 20mm (0.79in) Flak twin AA guns

Crew: 25

Type IID

The pressure hull's length was 29.8m (97.75ft), two thirds of total length, an indicator of the cramped internal conditions.

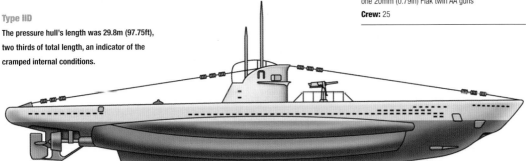

U-570, captured by the Royal Navy on 27 August 1941, is inspected by Royal Navy crew. The deck gun for the Type VIIC was an 8.8 centimetres (3.5in) quick-firing with about 220 rounds.

STANDARD GUNS AND MOUNTINGS ON U-BOATS

105mm (4.1in) SK C/32 U: Deck gun used on Types I and IX.

105mm (4.1in) SK L/45 on C/36 mounts, used on later Type X and Type XB.

88mm (3.4in) SK C/35: Widely used on Type VII, fitted on handworked single C35 mounts, sited either on the deck or on a raised platform.

37mm (1.4in) FlakM42U: An automatic model, seen only in the late stages of the war, it could fire 150–180 rounds per minute, mounted singly or as twin.

37mm (1.4in) SK C/30 U: Manually loaded, with a rate of fire of around 30 rpm. Fitted on a single C35 mounting.

20mm (0.79in) MG C30: Hand-worked by two men with a rate of fire of 280–300 rpm. Mounted singly in a watertight canister or on twin C33/27 mountings.

20mm (0.79in) Flak38: Improved version of the MG C30. Firing rate 450–500 rpm. At first worked from C 30/27 mountings, it was later also put on M43U twin mount (Flak-Zwilling) or the four-barrel 38/43U Flak-Vierling).

7.92mm (0.3in) MG C34: Modified version of the standard infantry machine gun, with rapid fire of 1000 rpm, but ineffective as an AA weapon.

Type VII (1935–45)

An effective hunter-killer in the first years of the war, the Type VII eventually fell victim to intensive anti-submarine warfare both from the surface and the air.

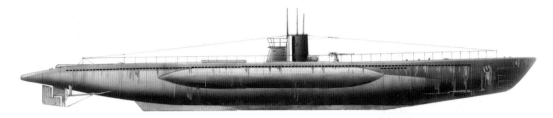

In production from 1935 to 1945, this was the most numerous submarine type ever built, with a total of 709 completed. The design group was headed by Friedrich Schürer, Germany's chief of submarine design from October 1939, and the prototype was the Finnish *Vetehinen* minelayer class of 1930, itself based on Germany's WWI UB-III type. The design was German and under a secret treaty between Germany and Finland, the three-strong class was used for training German submariners.

Type VIIA

Numbered U-27 to U-36, the first ten, VIIA, were built at AG Weser, Bremen, and Germaniawerft, Kiel. They were single-hulled, with bow and stern sections welded onto the cylindrical pressure hull. External blister tanks for main ballast and reserve fuel, regulating tanks and reserve buoyancy tanks were also welded on. The regulating tanks were pressure-proofed.

Initial production was slow, and only a few were combat-ready in September 1939. Operating range was 4300nm

U-32 (Type VIIA)

U-32 is shown during the Spanish Civil War, bearing the distinguishing stripes of the international 'Non-Interventionist Committee', patrolling shipping lanes off the Spanish coast, 1938–39.

U-32 (Type VIIA)

Dimensions: Length 64.5m (211.6ft), Beam 5.8m (19ft), Draught 4.4m (14.4ft)
Displacement (surface/submerged): 636 tonnes (626t) / 757 tonnes (745t)
Propulsion: two 1722.5kW (2310hp) diesels; two 559kW (750hp) electric motors, two screws
Speed (surface/submerged): 16kt (29.6kmh, 18.4mph) / 8kt (14.8kmh, 9.2mph)
Range (surface/submerged): 4300nm (7964km, 4949mi) at 12kt (22.2kmh, 13.8mph) / 90nm (166.7km, 103.6mi) at 4kt
Armament: five 533mm (21in) torpedo tubes; 11 torpedoes or 22 TMA/33TMB mines; one 88mm (3.4in) gun, one 20mm (0.79in) gun
Crew: 44

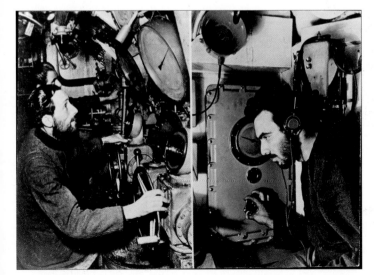

Crew at their stations monitor instumentation. Conditions in the U-boats were cramped and uncomfortable, ranging from stuffy tropical humidity to freezing Arctic temperatures, depending on the location of the boat.

(7964km, 4949mi). Operational depth was 100m (330ft). Despite its relatively large size, it could submerge within 30 seconds at neutral buoyancy, otherwise 50 seconds. Dive planes, fitted fore and aft, were operated either electrically or manually. The type was proven as the *Reichsmarine*'s first effective patrol boat, and already an improved version was being built.

The pressure hull was formed of three compartments separated by pressure-proof bulkheads and subdivided into six rooms by watertight bulkheads. It was formed of rolled, galvanized sheet steel varying in thickness from 185mm (7.3in) midships to 160mm (6.3in) towards the extremities. At the connection point of pressure hull and tower, the thickness increased to 220mm (8.58in). Plating

32mm (1.25in) thick was applied to the tower. The interior of the pressure hull, apart from the diesel engine room, had two levels, with working and living space on a deck above storage and bunkerage. The two central sections, containing the control room, a fridge and stores compartment, and the petty officers' quarters, were cylindrical, the others were truncated cones. The upper casing forming the deck was welded to the hull and topped with slatted wooden decking. Inside the casing were air trunks, aerials trunks, DF antenna, rod antenna, air search periscope, pressure-proof container for AA gun barrels, and the cooling water gravity tank. An inflatable dinghy was stowed in a compartment forward of the torpedo loading hatch. Net-cutting serrations were also applied to

Assembled U-boat crews and dock workers listen to an official address inside the pens at La Rochelle or St Nazaire, on the Atlantic coast of France.

the stem below the surface waterline. A Hall stockless anchor, 400kg (880lb), was fitted, with 150m (495ft) of chain and a compressed-air capstan.

Two six-cylinder MAN M6 V four-stroke 40/46 diesels provided main power, 1566–1722kW (2100–2310bhp), with two BBC (Brown Boveri Company) GG UB 7820/8 electric motors of 559kW (750hp). Battery power came from two AFA 62-cell sets: Type 27 MAK 40 in six of the VIIAs; Type 33 MAL 740 in the others. Compressed air was stored in 12 flasks with a total capacity of 3900m³ (137,727ft³). Fuel capacity in Type VIIA was 68 tonnes (67t), with

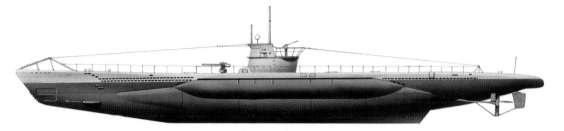

U-99 (Type VIIB)

U-99, commissioned on 18 April 1940, sank over 244,000 GRT of Allied shipping before being sunk by the destroyer HMS *Walker* on 17 March 1941.

59.5 tonnes (58.6t) inside the pressure hull. Four internal bow torpedo tubes were fitted, plus an external stern tube mounted on the after deck (this was discontinued in later VII types). Total warload was 11 torpedoes, or 22 TMA mines, or 33 TMB mines. External armament consisted initially of an 88mm (3.4in) C35 deck gun, partly protected by a breakwater, and a 20mm (0.79in) AA gun mounted at bridge deck level. Additionally, 205 rounds of deck gun ammunition were held.

Type VIIB

The Type VIIB numbered 24 boats, built at Germaniawerft, Bremer Vulkan and Flenderwerk in Lübeck. The dimensions were slightly increased, enabling a longer control room, and raising displacement to 765 tonnes (753t) / 871 tonnes (857t). The MAN diesel engines were uprated with exhaust-driven *Büchigebläse* supercharging to give a 1kt increase in surface speed: this was important for tactical positioning because most convoys moved at only 10–12kt. U-45–U-50 had Germaniawerft six-cylinder F46 four-stroke diesels giving 2088–2312kW (2800–3100bhp), supercharged mechanically from the drive shaft (*Kapselgebläse*). Reverse cams were provided with each engine, allowing slowing or (under suitable

MACHINERY

Throughout the war, German submarines were powered by direct drive. In this system, the diesel engine was directly coupled to the propeller shaft. A clutch between it and the combined electric motor/DC generator (MG) could be disengaged to let the MG alone drive the shaft. A second clutch aft of the MG enabled it to charge the batteries while the diesels turned the screws. German submarines retained the system in part because it was relatively compact and smaller submarines could be built in greater quantity; also, because while noisy from engine vibrations transmitted to the propeller, direct drive was more straightforward and cheaper to build and maintain.

VIICs U-82, 90 and 132–136 had two MAN single-acting M 6 V40/46 engines with forced induction by Büchi supercharger. Most VIIC had Germaniawerft-installed Krupp Model e.v. 40/46 with forced induction by Roots-type blower. Both types delivered 1044kW (1400shp). The MAN engine was slightly lighter and more compact, but performance was identical.

The batteries were Type 33 MAL 800 W, with 62 cells each, with a total weight of 62.1 tonnes (61.13t). The electric motors were mostly Brown Boveri (Mannheim) or AEG (Berlin), built to a standard pattern.

The engine room was the hottest place to work in a U-boat, and was especially cramped on the smaller Type II submarines.

U-47 (Type VIIB)

U-47 made world headlines and won glory in
Germany by a daring entry into the Scapa Flow
naval anchorage in the Orkney Islands on 14
October 1939, when it sank the battleship HMS
Royal Oak before making a successful getaway.

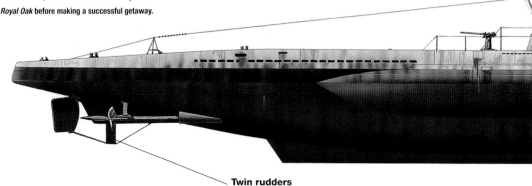

Twin rudders
Type VIIB had twin rudders
rather than the single rudder
of the VIIA boats, and its stern
tube was brought inside the
pressure hull.

U-47 (Type VIIB)

Dimensions: Length 66.5m (218ft), Beam 6.2m
(20.4ft), Draught 4.7m (15.4ft)

Displacement (surface/submerged):
765/871t (753/857 tons)

Propulsion: two 1722.5kW (2310hp) diesels; two
559kW (750hp) electric motors, two screws

Speed (surface/submerged): 16kt (29.6kmh,
18.4mph)/8kt (14.8kmh, 9.2mph)

Range (surface/submerged): 4300nm (7964km,
4949mi) at 12kt (22.2kmh, 13.8mph) / 90nm
(166.7km, 103.6mi) at 4kt

Armament: five 533mm (21in) torpedo tubes; 11
torpedoes or 22 TMA/33TMB mines; one 88mm (3.4in)
gun, one 20mm (0.79in) gun

Crew: 44

Surface camouflage
Colours of wartime U-boats varied
at different times, but were almost
always in shades of grey, usually
in two tones. Dunkelgrau 51 ('dark
grey', although actually more like
medium grey) above the surfaced
waterline, and *Schiffsbodenfarbe III
Grau* ('hull colour grey') below.

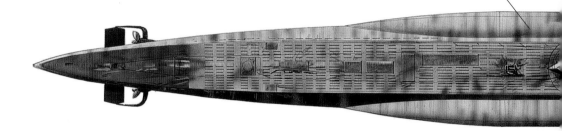

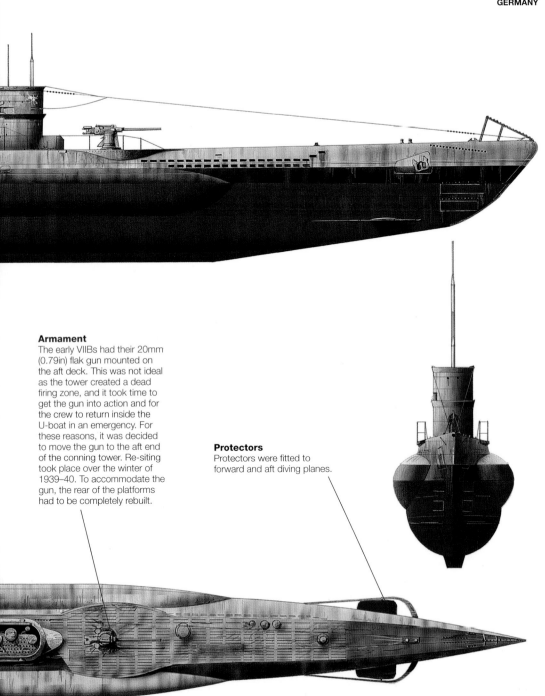

Armament
The early VIIBs had their 20mm (0.79in) flak gun mounted on the aft deck. This was not ideal as the tower created a dead firing zone, and it took time to get the gun into action and for the crew to return inside the U-boat in an emergency. For these reasons, it was decided to move the gun to the aft end of the conning tower. Re-siting took place over the winter of 1939–40. To accommodate the gun, the rear of the platforms had to be completely rebuilt.

Protectors
Protectors were fitted to forward and aft diving planes.

circumstances) reversing. All had AEG GU 460/6 278 electric motors, of the same power rating as on VIIA. Clutches between the diesel engines and the electric motors, and between the motors and the propellers, allowed several permutations of use for drive, charging or idling. Larger saddle tanks brought fuel capacity up to 110 tonnes (108.3t), enabling a range of 6500nm (12,038km, 7480mi). Twin rudders replaced the VIIA's single. The stern torpedo tube was moved inside the hull, with a reserve torpedo (U-83 had no stern tube). Fourteen torpedoes, 26 TMA, or 39 TMB

mines could be carried. Crew numbers were increased by four.

Type VIIC

The Type VIIC numbered 577 boats, with 17 shipyards sharing the building. The hull was further lengthened to allow for an active *S-Gerät* sonar installation which in the event was not ready in time. The tower was slightly widened and made 30cm (11.7in) longer. Fuel capacity was increased to 115 tonnes (113t), allowing an operating range of 8650nm (16,020km, 9954mi) at 12kt. With Type VIIC/41 (88 boats

from July 1943), built of higher-grade steel, operational depth was down to 120m (394ft). The 'knife-switch' electrical system inherited from WWI boats gave way to an AEG-designed 'knob-switch' system. Some Type VIIC had both electric and diesel air compressors. With so many boats, builders and repairers, the range of detail variations across the VIIC Type is

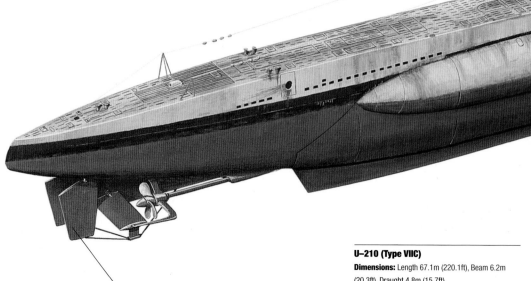

Propellers
The standard U-boat propellers were three-bladed, with a diameter of 1620mm (5.26ft).

U-210 (Type VIIC)

U-210 was a typical Type VIIC U-boat. Almost all U-boats carried their own emblem, painted on the tower. U-210's was a lobster, with claws extended in attacking mode.

U–210 (Type VIIC)

Dimensions: Length 67.1m (220.1ft), Beam 6.2m (20.3ft), Draught 4.8m (15.7ft)

Displacement (surface/submerged): 773.1 tonnes (761t) / 878.8 tonnes (865t)

Propulsion: two 2087kW (2800hp) diesels; two 559kW (750hp) electric motors, two screws

Speed (surface/submerged): 17.2kt (31.8kmh, 19.8mph) / 7.6kt (14kmh, 8.7mph)

Range (surface/submerged): 6500nm (12,038km, 7481mi) at 12kt (22.2kmh, 13.8mph) / 80nm (148km, 92mi) at 4kt

Armament: five 533mm (21in) torpedo tubes; 14 torpedoes or 26 TMA/39TMB mines; one 88mm (3.4in) gun, one 20mm (0.79in) gun

Crew: 44

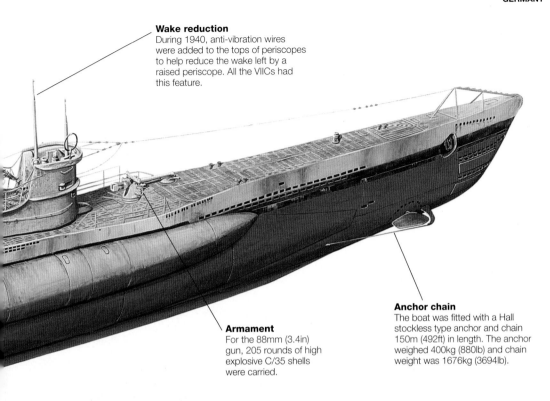

Wake reduction
During 1940, anti-vibration wires were added to the tops of periscopes to help reduce the wake left by a raised periscope. All the VIICs had this feature.

Armament
For the 88mm (3.4in) gun, 205 rounds of high explosive C/35 shells were carried.

Anchor chain
The boat was fitted with a Hall stockless type anchor and chain 150m (492ft) in length. The anchor weighed 400kg (880lb) and chain weight was 1676kg (3694lb).

TORPEDOES

German torpedoes manufactured during World War II were denoted as G, followed by designation of their diameter, length and propulsion. Thus, G7e T2 meant that the torpedo was 533mm (21in) in diameter, about 7m (23ft) long, had an electric motor and was the second modification to the original design. G7a was powered by a gas-steam (wet heater) system and replaced the compressed air-driven G7v. From late 1942, a pre-set guidance system, FaT ('spring apparatus torpedo') was introduced, developed in 1944 into LuT ('position-independent torpedo').

In May 1943 the war-load for a Type VIIC was: four G7a T I FaT I, six G7e T III and two G7e T III FaT II. From April 1944, it was five G7es TV (a new acoustic-homing model known as Zaunkönig, 'Wren'), five G7e LuT, or two G7e FaT I and three G7e FaT II.

The standard warhead held 280kg (617lb), its charge consisting of hexanite (HND), TNT, and powdered aluminium. Type V Zaunkönig had a 274kg (604lb) warhead.

One of the numerous publicity shots of Type VIIB U-47 on its return from sinking HMS *Royal Oak*.
Features of the tower include the spray deflector and the fixings of the net wire.

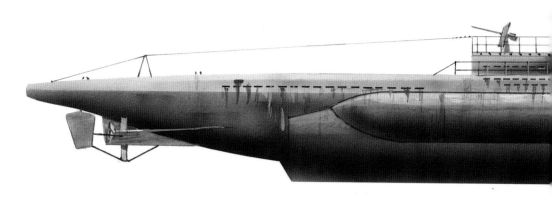

U-551 (Type VIIC)

Shown here with the central railing fitted for a time to some of
the class, U-551 was sunk off Iceland on its first patrol by the
ASW trawler *Visenda* on 23 March 1941.

U-533 (Type VIIC)

This profile of U-553 shows adaptation of the
VIIC for additional AA protection. The extended
platform carries a four-barrelled 'Flakvierling'
20mm (0.79in) gun.

U-320 (Type VIIC/41)

Type VIIC/41 had a stronger pressure hull enabling it to dive
operationally to 120m (394ft). Ninety were built in this form.
The hull of U-995 is preserved at Laboe, Germany.

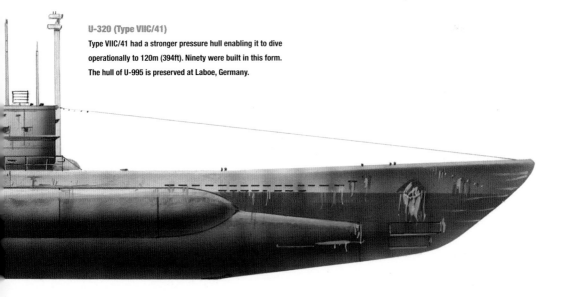

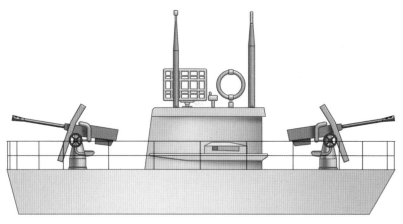

Wintergarten Flak platforms

Wintergarten normally referred to a small balcony in an apartment building, allowing plants to be kept and providing an open-air space. Its use to describe the Flak gun platform (and smoking area) on Type VII and IX U-boats was semi-humorous. Designed to maximize anti-aircraft power, the Turm VII conversion (illustrated) carried two pairs of powerful 3.7cm (1.5in) Flak guns.

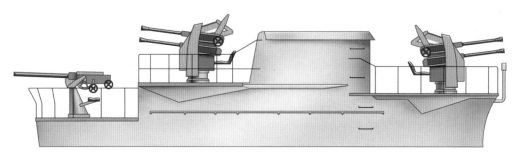

Enlarged Flak platform

Enlarged tower form of a Type VIIC 'Flakboot', 1943. Two quad 2cm (0.8in) Flakvierlings were mounted, together with a 3.7cm (1.5in) Flak gun. Although the Flak boats achieved some success, they could still be swamped by Allied fighter-bombers like the Mosquito, and the enlarged tower adversely affected both dive times and underwater handling.

Type VIIB raised platform

This AA gun configuration was tested on U-84, with a separate platform for a second 20mm (0.8in) gun aft of the tower. It was not adopted, but improved defence against aircraft was a constant concern.

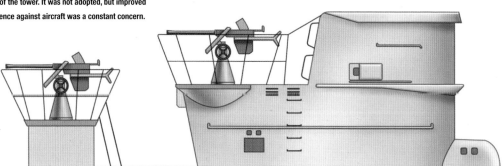

U-441 (Type VIIC)

In spite of her impressive anti-aircraft armament, U-441 was severely damaged on each of the patrols she mounted as a Flak boat, and she was converted back to normal Type VIIC configuration.

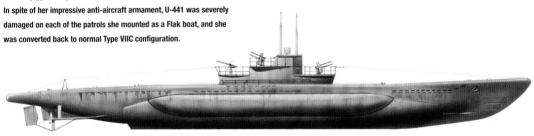

U-333 (Type VIIC)

U-333 was one of a number of boats newly equipped with a *Schnorchel* which were sent to try to interrupt the flow of supplies across the Channel after the Normandy invasion. It was the first boat to be sunk by the Squid ahead-throwing mortar.

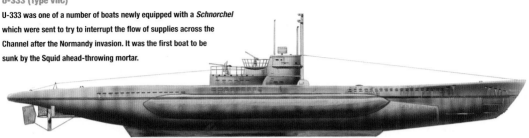

enormous, especially in armament and tower design. Most lost their deck gun by the end of 1942 when AA defence became more vital than surface attacks on smaller vessels, replaced by a twin 20mm (0.79in) mounting.

Flak boats

The *Wintergarten* platform built sternwards from below bridge level allowed for heavier fire, primarily from 20mm (0.79in) and 37mm (1.4in) Flak cannon, often in twin mountings. Snorkels became standard fittings from mid-1944. Four inflatable five-man life rafts were installed in canisters in the forward deck casing. Equipment included HF radio wire antenna, DF loop on retractable rotating antenna, active sonar, and echo depth sounders. Habitability of VIIC was slightly better than on previous U-boats (though it still shocked American, if not British,

sailors). A refrigerator could store fresh food for a time and provide ice.

Five VIIC were temporarily refitted as 'Flak boats' – requiring modification to the tower to allow for additional AA guns forward and aft, with a railed *Wintergarten* holding a 37mm (1.4in) gun and two quadruple 20mm (0.79in) guns. These were intended to increase protection for a group of surfaced boats, but there were practical difficulties, and all were back as regular VIIC by the end of 1943.

Type VIID

A further VII sub-class was formed by six minelayers (VIID) with five torpedo tubes and 15 mines of Type SMA – anchored magnetic, on cables from 400–600m (1320–1980ft) long and with a charge of 350kg (772lb), discharged from vertical tubes. This required an additional section 9.8m (32.1ft) long between frames 39 and 40. The extra

length also allowed for additional external fuel tanks, giving a range of 11,200nm (20,742km, 12,889mi) at 10kt. This sub-class and VIIF both had four forward and one stern torpedo tubes. Both were armed with one 37mm (1.4in) Flak gun and four 20mm (0.79in) C38 Flak guns in twin mountings.

Type VIIF

The four-strong Type VIIF was the largest of all the VII-class, 77.9m (255.5ft) long and with a beam of 6.38m (21ft). They were intended to supply torpedoes and other necessities to patrolling U-boats which had expended their stock. Apart from 14 torpedoes for their own use, they carried 24 for transfer in a cargo hold. By the time they were deployed in 1943, such transfer on the surface was impossibly hazardous. They were soon converted to transports.

Following its surrender, U-776 (Type VIIC), manned by a British crew, is shown off to the British public at Westminster Pier on the River Thames, London.

U-218 (Type VIID)

Able to lay as many as 15 large ground mines, U-218 mounted 10 patrols between 1942 and the end of the war. Only two ships were sunk by its weapons, one in the Clyde estuary and one in the Channel after the end of the war.

U-218 (Type VIID)

Dimensions: Length 44m (144.4ft), Beam 4.9m (16.8ft), Draught 3.9m (12.4ft)

Displacement (surface/submerged): 636 tonnes (626t) / 757 tonnes (745t)

Propulsion: two 1722.5kW (2310hp) diesels; two 559kW (750hp) electric motors, two screws

Speed (surface/submerged): 23.5/13.7km/hr (12.7/7.4kt) surf/sub

Surface range: 6389km (3450nm)

Armament: 14 torpedoes; 15 SMA mines in vertical chutes; 8.8cm SK C35 naval gun, with 220 rounds; two 2cm Flak C30 with 4,380 rounds

Crew: 46

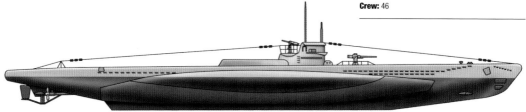

Type IX (1938–45)

Building on the lessons of Type IA, this was the *Kriegsmarine*'s prime ocean-going attack submarine.

Type IX was a great advance on IA, double-hulled, with a streamlined outer shell and an internal pressure hull formed of 18mm (0.7in) steel, divided into five compartments of cast steel 22mm (0.86in) thick. Openings in the pressure hull were: two torpedo hatches, one galley hatch, one engine room hatch, plus conning tower and periscope openings. Plating thickness on the tower was 40mm (1.18in). Enclosed in the outer hull were bow and stern buoyancy tanks, three main ballast tanks, five fuel ballast tanks, one fuel tank, two regulating variables (*Regelzelle* and *Regelbunker*), and one negative tank.

The tower was set aft of midships, with a long foredeck that helped in rapid diving. An extension aft of and below the bridge deck with its periscopes and snorkel held the

machine gun. There was room in the casing below the foredeck for ten torpedoes in pressurized containers.

Four bow tubes and two stern tubes were fitted, and the warload was 22 torpedoes. The first batch of Type IX, with U-37 as the lead ship, were armed with a 105mm (4.1in) deck gun, one 37mm (1.4in) AA cannon, mounted on the after deck, and one C/30 machine gun.

There were eight versions of Type IX, but the first four, IXA to IXC/40, had very similar vital statistics. All were powered by 1640.5kW (2200hp) MAN diesel engines, two SSW 373kW (500hp) electric motors and two 62-cell battery sets. Bunker capacity increased slightly in each revision with a consequent increase in surface range. Wartime modifications and repairs resulted in a variety of tower

---

U-37 (IXA)

Dimensions: Length 76.5m (251ft), Beam 6.5m (21.3ft), Draught 4.7m (15.42ft)

Displacement (surface/submerged): 1048.5 tonnes (1032t) / 1587.5 tonnes (1250t)

Propulsion: two 1640.5kW (2200hp) diesels; two 373kW (500hp); two screws

Speed (surface/submerged): 18.2kt (33.7kmh, 21mph) / 7.7kt (14.3kmh, 8.9mph)

Range: 8100nm (15,001km, 9323mi) at 12kt; 64nm (118.5km, 73.6mi) at 4kt

Armament: four bow, two stern 533mm (21in) torpedo tubes, 22 torpedoes. One 105mm (4.1in) deck gun, one 37mm (1.4in), one 20mm (0.79in) AA gun

Crew: 48

U-37 (Type IXA)

U-37 was the first of Type 1XA to be commissioned. Its 37mm (1.45in) AA gun was deck-mounted aft of the tower.

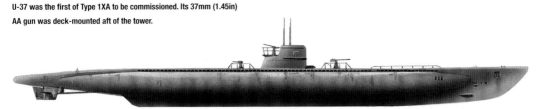

U-107 (Type IXB)

Although a part of 2. Flottille, U-107 took part in the attack on convoy HG 76. While unsuccessful in this operation, U-107 did sink 37 ships over the course of 14 patrols, making her one of the most successful U-boats of the war.

U-123 (Type IXB)

One of the most successful U-boats of the war, U-123 under her three Knight's Cross-winning commanders sank 42 merchant ships totalling 219,924 GRT, one auxiliary warship of 3209 GRT and the British submarine P615.

configurations. The foredeck gun was also removed in many cases.

Type IXB (16 boats)

Very like the first batch but had capacity for 167.6 tonnes (165t) rather than 154t of fuel, enabling a range of 12,000nm (22,224km, 13,809mi). Like Type IXA, three periscopes were fitted, one to the conning tower and two to the control room. The latter was dropped in later IX boats.

Type IXC (54 boats)

Bunkerage for 211 tonnes (208t) of oil. Surface range now extended to 11,000nm (20,372km, 12,659mi) at 12kt. The AA gun emplacement was

moved to a lower-level platform aft of the tower, with two torpedoes stored below. U-67 was used to trial the *Alberich* soundproofing coating. Other boats had modifications applied to deal with specific conditions, like reinforced bows for icy Arctic waters.

Type IXC/40 (87 boats)

Surface range extended to 11,400nm (21,113km, 13,119mi). The 105mm (4.1in) gun was removed and the single 20mm (0.79in) AA guns were replaced by twin mountings.

Type IXD (two boats)

Displacement increased to 1636 tonnes (1610t) / 1828 tonnes (1799t),

with length increased to 87.6m (287.4ft) beam to 7.5m (24.6ft), draught to 5.4m (17.7ft). Propulsion was by six Daimler-Benz MB-501 diesels (as used on E-boats), three on each shaft, giving 6711kW (9000hp) at 1600rpm, for a surface speed of 20.8kt. Submerged speed was slightly less than earlier IX types at 6.9kt (12.8kmh, 7.9mph). A Focke-Achgelis FA-330 manned observation kite was carried. The high-power engines were unsatisfactory and both boats were re-engined and converted to transports.

Type IXD Cargo (two boats)

Slowest of all the IX types, powered by two Germaniawerft (Krupp) diesels

Snorkel pipe
The snorkel pipe angled down into a horizontal recess on the forward starboard side of the tower. Fitting of a snorkel required removal of the forward deck gun. Previously this might have been a 105mm (4.1in) SK C/32 or a 37mm (1.5) single flak gun.

Extra torpedoes
Up to 24 torpedoes were carried, including four stored in upper deck containers, below the aft flak platform.

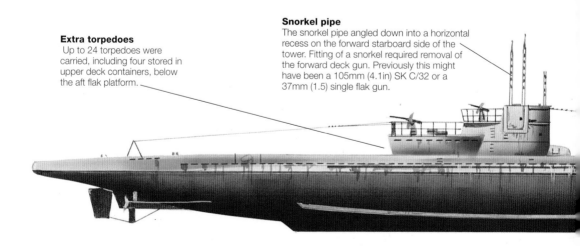

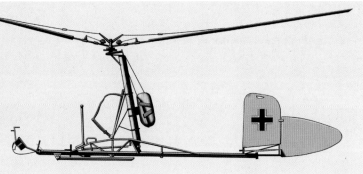

ROTARY KITE
U-boats deployed to the Far East were fitted with a Focke-Achgelis (Fa-330) unpowered rotary kite which could be unpacked and rigged on the deck, then towed on a 150m (495ft) cable, rising on the autogyro principle, and brought down by a winch. It gave a much wider 360° view than was obtainable from the bridge.

of 1044kW (1400hp) and two standard 373kW (500hp) electric motors, they made 15.8kt (29kmh, 18.2mph) surfaced). These had no torpedo armament but had space for 256 tonnes (252t) of supplies. They had the standard gun set and also a Focke-Achgelis FA-330 manned observation kite, stored in a cylindrical housing on the open deck.

Type IXD (2 boats)
The largest Type IX, of dimensions very close to the other IXDs, but with MAN 1640.5kW (2200hp) diesels

supplemented by MWM six-cylinder four-stroke RS34.5S engines of 432.5kW (580hp), enabling cruising speed while the main engines charged the batteries. Fuel capacity of 449 tonnes (442t) gave a surface range of 23,700nm (43,892km, 27,273mi) at 12kt. Eight vertical mine shafts, each with four mines, could replace the torpedo storage. After commissioning, a snorkel was fitted, the deck gun was removed, and the single 20mm (0.79in) AA cannon was changed to a twin mounting.

Snorkels were fitted to a number of Type IXs, requiring removal of three

stored torpedoes on the starboard side to accommodate the hinged pipe. Four of class IXC were equipped with a hinged 15m (49ft) radio mast for long-range communication, but it was later removed.

U-864 (Type IXD/2)
A long-range attack boat, commissioned in December 1943. U-864 was at the start of a mission from Norway to Japan, carrying canisters of metallic mercury in the keel duct, when it was tracked and sunk by a torpedo from V-class submarine HMS Venturer, with both boats submerged, on 9 February 1945.

Length
Type IXD/2 was 11.1m (36.4ft) longer than Type IXA, with a surface displacement of 1642 tonnes (1616t) compared to 1048.5 tonnes (1032t).

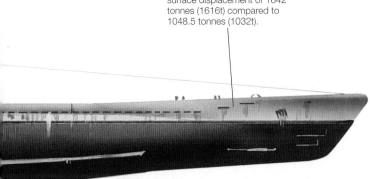

U-864 (IXD/2)
Dimensions: Length 76.5m (251ft), Beam 6.5m (21.3ft), Draught 4.7m (15.42ft)
Displacement (surface/submerged): 1048.5 tonnes (1032t)/1587.5 tonnes (1250t)
Propulsion: two 1640.5kW (2200hp) diesels; six-cylinder four-stroke RS34.5S outputting 432.5kW (580hp)
Speed (surface/submerged): 18.2kt (33.7kmh, 21mph) / 7.7kt (14.3kmh, 8.9mph)
Range: 23,700nm (43,892km, 27,273mi) at 12kt;
Armament: four bow, two stern 533mm (21in) torpedo tubes, 22 torpedoes. One 37mm (1.4in) gun, twin 20mm (0.79in) AA guns
Crew: 48

Type XIV (1941)

Known to the German submariners as *Milchkühe* (milk cows), this was a class of ten supply boats intended to refuel and restock U-boats on ocean patrol.

Consideration of a 'submarine' tanker went back to the 1930s, though specifications for the Type XIV were not drawn up until 1940 when the U-boat fleet was ranging far out into the Atlantic in pursuit of British convoys. Features of the Types VII and IX were incorporated in the design, but the XIV did not share their hull shape, which was of similar length but greater in beam and depth, reflecting its cargo-carrying task. It had a flat open deck to cope with the always tricky business of boat-to-boat transfer. It was double-hulled, with tankage for 432 tonnes (425t) of fuel oil and 13 tonnes (12.8t) of lubricating oil between the inner and outer hulls. The tower and bridge were modelled on the Type IX, though details of the aft gun platform varied in different Type XIV boats. All were built in Kiel, U-459 to U-464 at the Deutsche Werke yard and U-487 to U-490 at Germaniawerft. Inside the pressure hull was a double-deck layout, with cargo storage compartments where up to 20 tonnes (19.7t) of supplies could be held on pallets, ready for transfer. Fully loaded, the Type XIV could extend the patrol period of 12 Type VII U-boats for four weeks.

Type XIV could travel at a depth of 150m (492ft) thanks to a pressure hull of 251mm (0.98in) steel, useful for a

U-459 (Type XIV)

Dimensions: Length 67.10m (220.2ft), Beam 9.35m (30.8ft), Draught 6.51m (21.4ft)

Displacement (surface/submerged): 1688 tonnes (1661t) / 1932 tonnes (1901t)

Propulsion: two 1640.5kW (2200hp) diesels; two 373kW (500hp) electric motors; two screws

Speed (surface/submerged): 14.9kt (27.6kmh, 17.1mph) / 6.2kt (11.5kmh, 7.1mph)

Range (surface/submerged): 12,350nm (22,872km, 14,212mi) at 10kt / 55nm (102km, 63mi) at 4kt

Armament: two 37mm (1.4in) guns, one 20mm (0.79in) AA gun

Crew: 53

U-461 (Type XIV)

The concept of the U-boat feeder, able to avoid detection until it reached a meeting point, was effective until the German radio codes were broken and their missions ceased to be secret. The system then had to be abandoned.

U-459 (Type XIV)

U-459, first of the 10 boats of Type XIV, was the *Kriegsmarine*'s first purpose-built refuelling and supply submarine, a large boat intended to intensify the Atlantic war by enabling attack vessels to spend longer periods at sea.

submarine with no torpedo armament (it carried four for transfer). It has been suggested that it could go as deep as 240m (790ft). Its engines were the same as used in Types VII and IX, 1640.5kW (2200hp) MAN diesel engines, two SSW 373kW (500hp) electric motors and two 62-cell battery sets. Its own fuel supply was 181 tonnes (178t).

The boats were fitted with the necessary pipes and tackle for oil transfer. The feeding boat would be taken in tow and the fuel line floated back, with a telephone line. A calm sea was highly desirable. Both boats ran on their electric motors to keep station. The whole process could take several hours. The final boat in the class, U-490, was experimentally fitted with underwater refuelling tackle.

Davits could be rigged at the deck hatches, but these were often unusable because of the Type XIV's low freeboard, and stores were then passed using either the XIV's 6m (19.7ft) inflatable dinghy or by a line

passed between the boats (alongside at a safe distance for this exercise). Transfer of torpedoes, almost 6m (20ft) long and weighing around 700kg (1540lb) was the hardest task, though the Type IXs had their own deck-handling equipment. The *Milchkühe* provided freshly-baked bread, refrigerated foodstuffs and had a doctor on board.

For air defence, the ten boats of the class originally had two quick-firing 37mm (1.4in) cannon, one forward and one aft of the bridge, and a 20mm (0.79in) on a raised platform attached to the tower. This was reinforced in 1943 with a second, lower platform aft, mounting either a single 37mm (1.4in) cannon or quadruple 20mm (0.79in) 'Vierling' guns.

Despite this, a combination of intensive air attacks and the Allies' ability to decode German radio messages and arrange interception, made the Type XIV's role unsustainable. All ten were sunk, mostly by air attack.

The transfer operation, in anything other than a flat calm, was a tricky business. A Type VIIB is being refuelled while another waits.

ACOUSTIC PROTECTION
Alberich was the code name of the anechoic acoustic protection system developed from 1940. Synthetic rubber tiles were applied to the outer hull surface. These muffled the submarine's sonar signature in the 10–18 kHz range by up to 15 per cent. The tiles were 4mm (0.2in) thick and there was great difficulty in finding a binding adhesive. Tested on U-67 (IXC), more than half its coating disappeared on its first voyage. It was 1944 before an adequate adhesive was found and used with considerable success on U-480 (VIIC) until its sinking on 24 February 1945. But it never went into general use.

Type XB (1942–45)

The Type XB were the *Kriegsmarine's* largest U-boats, used as minelayers, supply boats and transports.

A specialized minelayer type was required to plant larger mines than could be ejected from a 533mm (21in) tube. Type XA never went beyond the design stage; the first Type XB, U-116, was commissioned in July 1941. All eight of the class were built by Germaniawerft in Kiel. Fully double-hulled, its pressure hull was divided into five compartments by four pressure-proof bulkheads and into seven rooms separated by two watertight bulkheads. The pressure hull was built from rolled steel plates in tapering thickness of 20.5mm (0.8in) to 17mm (0.66in) from midships to the ends, with 88 inner frames set approximately 800mm (31in) apart. Six vertical mineshafts were placed forward, their caps rising above deck level. Each held three SMA mines in wet storage. On each side were twelve shorter shafts each holding two mines. Behind these, with no forward torpedo tubes, crew space was unusually generous, as the dimensions of the boat allowed for a two-deck arrangement. The control room was below the tower, with two periscopes. Officers' and petty officers' accommodation was forward and aft of it. Aft of the motor room were two stern-facing torpedo tubes. Between the hulls, apart from main ballast tanks,

were supplementary diving tanks, fuel tanks, and storage for six torpedoes (accessible only when surfaced). A further five were held inboard, including two in the tubes.

Propulsion was by two Germaniawerft nine-cylinder four-stroke F46a-9pu supercharged diesels each of a maximum 1790kW (2400hp) and two AEG double GU720/8-287 410kW (550hp) electric motors. Fuel capacity was 374 tonnes (368.2t). The two battery sets, AFA 124-cell 33MAL 800W, were as usual in compartments placed low in the hull.

The torpedo tubes were for defence, as the stern location suggests, with a generous nine reloads. Surface weaponry was one 105mm (4.1in)/45cal deck gun on the foredeck, one 37mm (1.4in) aft of the tower, and one 20mm (0.79in) AA gun mounted aft of the bridge. From 1943, the forward gun was removed and the 20mm (0.79in) gun was replaced by a twin mounting.

External work and rescue equipment included two signal buoys, three lifebuoys, 72 sets of emergency escape gear, 55 life jackets, two diving suits (one with weighing systems), a watertight suit for the emergency escape set, two life-rafts and an inflatable dinghy.

U118 (Type XB)

Dimensions: Length 89.8m (294.6ft), Beam 9.2m (30.2ft), Draught 4.7m (15.4ft)

Displacement (surface/submerged): 1791.2 tonnes (1763t) / 2212 tonnes (2177t)

Propulsion: two 1790kW (2400hp) diesels, two 410kW (550hp) electric motors, two screws

Speed (surface/submerged): 16.4kt (29.8kmh, 18.9mph) / 7kt (13kmh, 8mph)

Range (surface/submerged): 14,450nm (26,761km, 16,632mi) at 12kt / 188nm (348km, 216.4mi) at 2kt

Armament (original): 66 SMA mines, one 105mm (4.1in) gun, one 37mm (1.4in), one 20mm (0.79in) AA gun

Crew: 52

U-118 (Type XB)

The largest submarines in service with the *Kriegsmarine* during World War II, the Type XB boats could carry 66 mines. However, the class handled poorly and its slow diving time meant that it was vulnerable to air attack.

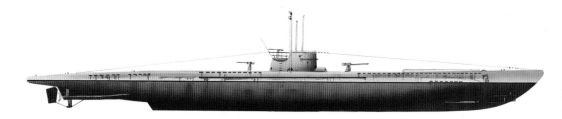

Aircraft from USS *Bogue* (CVE-9) attack U-118 with depth charges and machine guns while the U-boat is surfaced somewhere in the Atlantic. U-118's wake suggests it has been evading, but to no avail.

Some of the class were adapted or converted. U-119 was fitted as a supply ship with cradles for eight torpedoes and acted as a fuel supplier while retaining its capacity as a minelayer. U-219 and the last of the type, U-234, were turned into long-range cargo carriers for communication with Japan. The lateral mine shafts were removed and replaced by cargo holds, while the forward shafts were used to hold cylindrical containers. U-234's first trip coincided with the end of the war in Europe, and on surrender, it was found to have containers of uranium oxide in its forward shafts.

GERMAN MINES

Type TM (*Torpedomine*) fired from 533mm (21in) torpedo tubes, was self-anchoring. TMA, with a cable and a buoyancy chamber, could be laid two at a time in depths down to 270m (880ft). Its warhead weighed 230kg (507lb). TMB lay on the seabed in water 22–27m (72–90ft) deep, with a charge of 420–560kg (926–1235lb). It was 2.3m (7.6ft) long and could be laid three at a time. Both were magnetic influence mines with cylindrical aluminium alloy cases. In 1940 Type TMC was introduced: a seabed mine with a charge of 860–930kg (1896–2050lb) and a functional depth down to 37m (120ft). It could be fitted with magnetic or acoustic fuses.

Type XB U-boats carried SM (*Schachtmine*) type, with a diameter of 1.33m (4.4ft), discharged from non-pressurized shafts. SMA was moored to a depth of 250m (880ft). Type EMS was a surface floating mine designed to sink within 72 hours. It had a relatively small charge, 14kg (31lb). Type MTA was a modified torpedo, which could be preset to run for up to 7000m (7655yd), then sink to the seabed. Maximum effective depth was 20m (66ft). All could be detonated by magnetic or acoustic sensors.

Type XXI (1943–45)

The '*Elektroboot*' heralded a new generation of combat submarines. This was a 'stopgap' design in Grand Admiral Dönitz's strategic view.

German scientists and naval architects, led by Dr Helmuth Walter, were working on a 'true' submarine design that could run submerged for days rather than hours and would be virtually undetectable. But that was still a good way off. The Type XXI was intended to fill the gap. The urgent need for such a submarine, and confidence in the design, meant that 118 were ordered without a prototype to test. It incorporated many of Walter's ideas.

Streamlined hull

The streamlined outer hull covered a pressure hull in figure-of-eight form, one larger chamber above the other, formed from a steel/aluminium alloy 26mm (1in) thick in the wider central area, and 18mm (0.7in) towards the ends. This hull had an estimated crush depth of 340m (1110ft) and permitted diving to 280m (919ft), far below any previous limit. U-2506 is known to have dived to at least 220m (720ft). Construction was modular, in three stages, with nine prefabricated sections – eight hull modules plus the tower and pressurized 'conning tower' inner

chamber – formed at inland sites and transferred by barge to shipyards for a fitting out stage where the interior equipment of each module was installed. The final stage, carried out at the Blohm & Voss (Hamburg), AG Weser (Bremen) and Schichau (Danzig/Gdansk) yards, was to join and weld together all the modules. This process was to enable the 118 boats to be constructed within an unusually short time: a plan that did not work well in practice, with varying standards of welding and delivery of sections with imperfect fit.

Smooth lines

The tower was of a new, streamlined design with the tower above the control room. The bridge was minimal: this boat was meant to be operated from below the surface. Type XXI's smooth lines made existing submarines look antique: everything – guns, aerials, bollards – was retractable (including the bow diving planes) to ensure minimum drag in the water.

A single large rudder was fitted aft of the propellers. Internally it was divided into six compartments between the

---

U-3001 (Type XXI)

Dimensions: Length 76.7m (251.8ft), Beam 8m (26.3ft), Draught 6.32m (20.75ft)

Displacement (surface/submerged): 1621 tonnes (1595t) / 1819 tonnes (1790t)

Propulsion: two 1640.5kW (2200hp) diesels; two 1864kW (500hp) electric motors; two 241kW (323hp) creep motors; two screws

Speed (surface/submerged): 15.6kt (28.9kmh, 18mph) / 17.2kt (31.9kmh, 19.8mph)

Range (surface/submerged): 11,150nm (20,650km, 12,831mi) at 12kt / 285nm (528km, 328mi) at 6kt

Armament: Six 533mm (21in) torpedo tubes, two twin 20mm (0.79in) Flak mountings

Crew: 57

U-2501 (Type XXI)

Streamlining of the hull and tower helped to make this the first submarine to travel faster underwater than on the surface.

GERMAN SONAR

A GHG (*Gruppenhorchgerät*: grouped listening apparatus) was first installed in U-boats in 1935. It originally had two fixed sets of hydrophones (11, later 24) mounted below the bow but went through modifications. The KDB *Kristaldrehbasisgerät* type used receivers on a rotatable T-form mount placed forward of tubes and anchor capstan, rising 40cm (15.6in) above the deck. The *Balkongerät* was a larger and more effective version of the GHG, covering an underwater arc of around 1700. It was fitted to Type XXI and to some Type VII in 1944–45. VIIC boats were also fitted with *Sondergerät* (Special active sonar apparatus), transmitting pulses and analyzing the echoes. But it also advertised the U-boat's presence.

bow and stern sections, separated by pressure bulkheads.

Main engine

Walter's ultimate aim was for an air-independent main engine, but he had to compromise with two MAN M6V409/46KBB supercharged six-cylinder diesels delivering 2900kW (3900hp). The exhaust-driven supercharger did not work well and was removed, reducing the power output. But the battery size was three times that of the Type IX, arranged port and starboard in sets of three, each in three separate battery rooms. The 372 cells were AFA 4MAL740E. Altogether the installation weighed almost 243 tonnes (239t). It drove two SSW GU365/30 double-acting electric motors delivering 3700kW (4900hp), propelling Type XXI faster underwater than many ASW ships on the surface. Each shaft also had an SSW GV232/28 silent creep motor. Gears and clutches connected main motors to shafts, V-belts for the

Torpedo warheads being prepared before loading at a German U-boat base.

FIRE CONTROL

Systems became increasingly sophisticated. U-boats were equipped with TRW (*Torpedorichtungweiseranlage*) from 1942. Incorporating a UZO optic aiming device and transmitter coupled to the periscope, it could identify the angle of fire towards up to five moving ships in a convoy, within a few seconds. Designated T.Vh.Re.3 by Siemens, it enabled aiming and bearing target transmission, also electro-mechanical TDC (torpedo data control) which calculated the gyro angle and torpedo spread angle; and transmitted shot and spread angles direct to the torpedoes' gyroscopes. Firing could be done from the bridge or the control room.

creep motors. Fuel capacity was 228 tonnes (224.3t). The three-bladed propellers were of standard design.

The speed of design and production meant that many modifications had to be made, often requiring retrofitting. One major change was the incorporation of a snorkel. Extensive use of hydraulic power included torpedo reloading and a periscope ram. An emergency steering mechanism was fitted close to the stern.

Armament

Six torpedo tubes, all forward-facing, were fitted, and 17 reload torpedoes were carried. Alternatively, the Type XXI could hold 14 torpedoes and 12 TMC mines. The part-automated torpedo reload system enabled three salvoes of six torpedoes to be fired within 20 minutes. The AA guns were housed within the streamlined tower but otherwise of standard type, two twin 20mm (0.79in) C/30.

Air intake

Despite its advantages, the snorkel needed to be used with care. The intake pipe drew in air for the crew as well as the engines, letting the entire hull volume act as an air buffer. If the valve was suddenly closed, the diesels could run on for a short time, but would use all internal air, with fatal consequences for the crew.

Type XXI

The cutaway profile of a Type XXI displays its revolutionary design and systems.

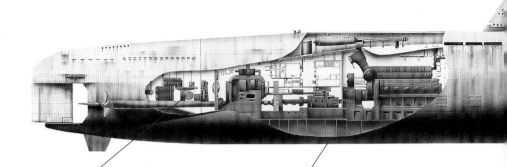

Back-up controls

An emergency steering wheel in the aftermost compartment could operate the single rudder.

Passive/active sonar

In the Type XXI an improved *Gruppenhorchgerät* (GHG) passive sonar system fitted beneath the keel, and a new active system, *Unterwasser-Ortungsgerät Nibelung*, enabled detection and attack of enemy shipping without optical contact – another revolutionary feature.

Advanced electronics were incorporated. The radar system was FuMB Ant 3 Bali (with antenna fixed on the snorkel head) and FuMO 65 Hohentwiel U1 with a Type F432 D2 series transmitter. Passive sonar of *Gruppenhorchgerät* (GHG) type was fitted at the keel, with the latest Unterwasser Ortungsgerät Nibelung non-line-of-sight active sonar sending data direct to the torpedo room.

Limited accommodation

The amount of technical equipment packed into the hull meant that only 47 berths were available for a crew of 57. Hammock hooks were provided. Nevertheless, it had air conditioning and crews were reported as regarding the new boats as 'palatial' compared with their predecessors.

Evasion tactics

Though the Type XXI would attack at slow speed, with the listening gear unaffected by its own propeller noise, it would use high speed to evade escort hunts. Its manoeuvrability (despite a large, submerged turning circle of 450m (1500ft) would pose difficulties for a single escort trying to hold contact, and several escort vessels might be needed to hem it in. Depth charge attacks would be wholly ineffective if the U-boat got any warning of the attack. Escorts fitted with forward-thrown weapons, such as Hedgehog and Squid, would fare better, although with the relatively short, fixed range at which these could be fired, and the rapid changes in bearing of a high-speed U-boat making evasion, accurate attacks were difficult to achieve. In addition, a *U-Bauer Boldschleuse* (decoy ejector) system in the stern compartment could emit bubbles and oil to make pursuers think the submarine had been sunk.

Streamlining
All external mountings were retractable when submerged. The 20mm (0.8in) flak guns were in streamlined housings on the tower (actually designed for 30mm/1in cannon.

Radar
Radar equipment was a FuMB Ant 3 Bali radar detector and antenna and a FuMO 65 Hohentwiel U1 radar with Type F432 D2 transmitter.

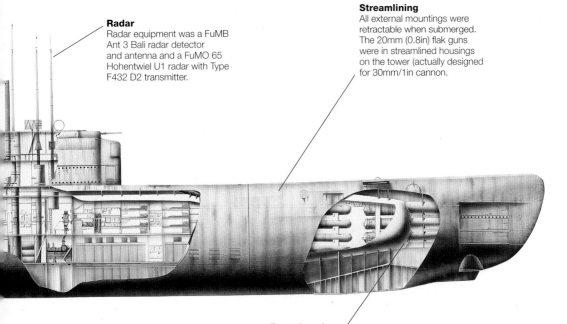

Torpedo salvo
Once a Type XXI had located a convoy, data collected by sonar was to be converted and automatically set in the new LUT (*Lageunabhängiger* Torpedo) torpedoes, which were then fired in spreads of six. This guided torpedo could be fired regardless of the target's bearing and steer an interception course programmed by the torpedo computer. The probability of hits on targets longer than 60m (200ft) was calculated at 95 per cent.

Type XXIII (1943–45)

This urgently needed coastal patrol submarine shared many characteristics of the Type XXI.

U-2321, the class leader, was laid down on 10 March 1944 and commissioned on 12 June that year – an indication of high priority and modular assembly, as with the Type XXI. A Helmuth Walter design, brought into production after several prototypes using Walter's hydrogen-peroxide fuel propulsion system had been tried and rejected, it was put together on the launch berth from four prefabricated sections. The lead contractor was Deutsche Werft in Hamburg. A small boat of only 237.7 tonnes (234t) surface displacement, it was packed with up-to-date equipment, including a substantial 62-cell battery set. The all-welded single hull was dismantlable into four parts, plus the tower, in order to be carried by rail to Black Sea or Mediterranean ports. In a boat only 34.7m (113ft) long fitted with two 7m (23ft) launch tubes, there was no space for internal loading and each tube carried a single torpedo. These were also novel – 'swim-out' tubes from which the electric-drive torpedo exited silently under its own power. Ballast tanks to hold 42.6 tonnes (42t) of water and bunkering for 18.3 tonnes (18t) of fuel oil also had to be fitted in.

The streamlined hull formation was designed for submerged speed and silence. In cross-section, the forward part of the hull was of expanded figure-of-eight form, with the tubes above and the battery compartment in a narrower lower section. The central part of the hull was a cylinder.

The tower was teardrop-shaped, tapering to a point, as did the stern. A single periscope was fitted at the back of the tiny open bridge, with the snorkel, its tube, like the periscope, inside the tower casing. *Balkongerät* detection apparatus was fitted under the bow. Originally no forward hydroplanes were fitted, but it was found necessary to install these for efficient diving.

The machinery had to be as compact as possible: a single MWM

U-2326

The small Type XXIII boat had a short range and was lightly armed, but its high underwater speed made it a potentially deadly opponent in coastal waters. U-2326 survived the war, surrendering at Dundee on 14 May 1945.

U-2326 (Type XXIII)

Dimensions: Length 34.68m (113.8ft), Beam 3.02m (9.9ft), Draught 3.66m (12ft)

Displacement (surface/submerged): 237.7 tonnes (234t) / 262 tonnes (258t)

Propulsion: 469.8kW (630hp) diesel; 426.5kW (572hp) electric motor; creep motor of 26kW (35hp), single screw

Speed (surface/submerged): 9.7kt (18kmh, 11mph) / 12.5kt (23kmh, 14.4mph)

Range (surface/submerged): 2600nm (4815km, 2992mi) at 8kt / 194nm (359km, 223mi) at 4kt

Armament: two bow torpedo tubes

Crew: 14

PERISCOPES

U-boats had night and attack periscopes, both being telescopic optical tubes within a stainless-steel pipe, raised electrically or hydraulically. The night type was NLSR C/9 (Nacht-LuftzielSehrohr). The types StaSR C/2 (Stand-Sehrohr) general purpose and attack ASR (Angriff-Seerohr) C/12 or C/13 periscope were located in the conning tower. On the periscope casing, directly over the ocular, an indicator was fitted, making it possible to read the current bearing without looking through the periscope. Type XXIII had a single shorter version of the ASR.

GERMAN RADAR

Radar was first installed in U-boats in 1942. It was FuMO-29 (*Funkmessortungsgerät*) surface and air search and required an array of dipoles around the bridge front. Also known as Seetakt, it was fitted to some Type VII and IXs. FuMO-30 followed, using a retractable, rotatable tube-shaped antenna on the port side of the bridge. In 1944 FuMO-61 Hohentwiel-U with a frame antenna 1.5m (4.9ft) by 1m (3.3ft) was fitted to 64 Type VII and IX. It was air-surface search: 20km (12.4mi) air and 7km (4.3mi) surface. More advanced versions were produced for Type XXI, including air-warning FuMO-391 Lessing, with the antenna on the snorkel mounting. But active radar played a much smaller part in the U-boats' actions than sonar.

Radar countermeasures began in August 1942 with the cumbersome FuMB-1 (*Funkmessbeobachtungsgerät*), using a makeshift antenna. The *Kriegsmarine* struggled throughout the war to find methods of countering the increasingly sophisticated radar detection abilities of the Allies. By the end of the war, some U-boats had three separate systems, set to different frequencies, all of whose antennas had to be taken down from the bridge before the boat could dive: FuMB-9 Zypern, FuMB-10 Borkum, and FuMB-7 Naxos. Others were in development as the war in Europe ended.

RS-348 469.8kW (630hp) diesel and an AEG GU 4463/8 426.5kW (572hp) electric motor. A creep motor was also fitted, a 26kW (35hp) BBC GCR-188 single-commutator turning the shaft by a belt reduction system to provide silent movement at 4.5kt. Like the Type XXI, it was faster when submerged.

No guns

The Type XXIII carried no guns and presumably relied on its nine-second crash-diving ability to avoid aerial attack – it could go down to 180m (594ft). The operational Type XXIIIs were appreciated by crews for their manoeuvrability both on the surface and submerged. While the surface speed was moderate, the submerged speed of 12.5kt could get them out of depth charge attacks, assuming the boat was detected. The principal shortcoming was that with an operational range of 4450nm (8241km, 5121mi), and good potential endurance, it only had two torpedoes to fire. On the other hand, its capacity to attack and the accuracy of its targeting gave a high chance of successful hits.

This would have been the largest class of submarines ever if the original plan for 980 had been fulfilled. As it was, only 61 were completed, of which six made operational patrols.

TYPE XXVII 'SEEHUND'

This was Germany's final version of the midget submarine, a two-man vessel 12m (39.4ft) long and 1.7m (5.6ft) in beam, carrying two G7e torpedoes. In total, 285 were built, and several are preserved in German museums today.

Pisani and Mameli classes (1925–28)

Unlike most other navies, the *Regia Marina* had a large and relatively up-to-date submarine arm in 1939.

These two very similar classes, though from separate design studios, set the pattern for future development of the submarine force. At this time the Italian Navy was in experimental mode, and these were intermediate in size, with potential use either as coastal or ocean-going boats. Only small classes were being built, and lengthy building times meant that an improved or adapted version was sometimes laid down before its predecessor was launched.

The double hull concept had originated in Italy, and both classes had this feature. Also typical was the large tower, which persisted on Italian boats despite its prominence as a target and its contribution to surface instability and underwater resistance. Bulges fitted to the outer hull sections helped stability but slowed surface speed to 15kt. This was rectified by re-engining surviving *Mameli* boats with 2982kW (4000hp) diesels in 1942.

SS *Mameli*, August 1944.

Giovanni Bausan (Pisani class)

Dimensions: Length 68.2m (223.9ft), Beam 6m (20ft), Draught 4.9m (16.2ft)

Displacement (surface/submerged): 894 tonnes (880t) / 1075 tonnes (1058t)

Propulsion: two diesels, 1118.5kW (1500hp), two 410kW (550hp) electric motors, two screws

Speed (surface/submerged): 15kt (27.8kmh, 17.3mph) / 8.2kt (15.2kmh, 9.4mph)

Range (surface/submerged): 5000nm (9260km, 5755mi) at 8kt / 61nm (113km, 70mi) at 4kt

Armament: six 533mm (21in) torpedo tubes, nine torpedoes; one 102mm (4in) deck gun, two single 13.2mm (0.5in) machine guns

Crew: 49

Giovanni Bausan

The *Pisani* class suffered from instability problems, which were partly rectified by fitting bulges to the bows, but this, and their obsolescent design, meant that little use was made of them as combat boats in World War II. *Des Geneys* was used as a battery-charging hulk and *Marcantonio Colonna* was broken up in 1943. Only *Vettor Pisani* survived the war. *Giovanni Bausan* was converted to an oil barge in spring 1942.

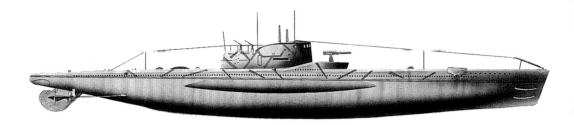

MINELAYING

The *Regia Marina* laid almost 55,000 mines during 1940–43, using surface vessels as well as submarines. The mines carried by the Foca-class were Types 150 and 150/1935 with warheads of 120 or 150kg (265–331lb), and Type 200, with a 200kg (441lb) warhead. This had a diameter of 1.17m (46in) and weighed 1150kg (2535lb). Mooring cables were up to 300m (990ft) long.

Mines were manufactured by the Pignone and Tosi companies, and the types were accordingly prefixed P- or T-. All were contact mines using the 'Hertz horn' detonator.

The *Bragadin* class consisted of just two submarines, including the *Filippo Corridoni* illustrated here, and were essentially minelaying versions of the earlier *Pisani* class. Mines were carried in two tubes. Seventeen different mine types were used by Italy, plus German versions. Some 54,457 were laid, mostly of moored types, accounting for 32 vessels, including 11 submarines.

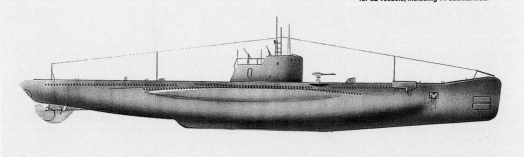

Giovanni da Procida (Mameli class)

Dimensions: Length 64.6m (212ft), Beam 6.51m (21.4ft), Draught 4.3m (14.1ft)

Displacement (surface/submerged): 823 tonnes (810t) / 1009 tonnes (993t)

Propulsion: two diesels, 1156kW (1550hp), two 410kW (550hp) electric motors, two screws

Speed (surface/submerged): 15kt (28kmh, 17mph) / 8kt (15kmh, 9.2mph)

Range (surface/submerged): 4360nm (8075km, 5017mi) at 8kt / 110nm (200km, 130mi) at 3kt

Armament: six 533mm (21in) torpedo tubes, 10 torpedoes; one 102mm (4in) deck gun, two single 13.2mm (0.5in) machine guns

Crew: 49

The main external difference was that the *Mameli* boats' 102mm (4in) gun was mounted on a low breakwater platform. This class, built at the Tosi yard in Taranto, was powered by two Franco Tosi four-stroke S8 eight-cylinder diesels developing 1156kW (1550hp). As well as the drive and the CGE electric motors, they were directly connected to a four-stage air compressor working at 70kg/cm^2

(995.6psi) to blow the ballast tanks and which also (in reverse) started the engines. The air intake valve for the diesels was placed quite low on the tower. The *Pisani* class, built at the Triestino yard, had greater fuel capacity than the *Mameli*, giving it a surface range of 5000nm (9260km, 5755mi) at 8kt, compared to 4360nm (8075km, 5017mi). Both had the same operational depth, 90m (300ft).

Giovanni da Procida

Despite its age and obsolescence *Giovanni da Procida* was on active service until January 1942 and was stricken only in 1948.

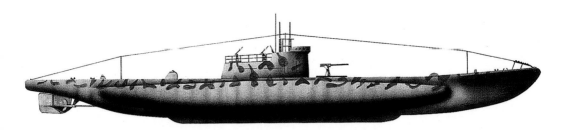

Balilla and Calvi classes (1927 and 1935)

Based on the German UEII type of WWI, *Balilla* was built by the OTO (Odero-Terni-Orlando) yard at La Spezia for long-range work in patrolling the coasts of African territories controlled by Italy.

Design and construction were to established standards. Double-hulled, its robust pressure hull enabled diving to 122m (350ft), deeper than any other submarine of the period. Its machinery was placed further forward than in other Italian submarines, but it had poor stability on the surface.

The class was powered by two Fiat diesels for surface cruising and two Savigliano electric motors for use while submerged. These developed 3700kW (4900hp) and 1600kW (2200hp) respectively. An auxiliary 317kW (425hp) diesel engine was also installed, enabling the boats to travel at full speed on the surface while still re-charging the batteries.

Unusually, the forward 120mm (4.7in)/27cal gun, large for a submarine,

was enclosed in a protective shield forward of the tower. This was replaced by an open-mounted 45cal type in 1934. At that time too the tower was reduced in size. Two twin 13.2mm (0.5in) machine guns were mounted on the tower abaft the bridge. One boat of the class, *Antonio Sciesa*, was modified to carry four mines in a discharge tube.

Calvi class

The three *Calvi* class, built by Odero-Terni-Orlando at Genoa, were essentially an improved version of *Balilla*, with complete double hulls. Its diesels, like *Balilla*'s, were Fiat; the electric motors were built by San Giorgio of Genoa. Two extra stern tubes were fitted, with a second gun mounted abaft the tower. Bolted on

Enrico Toti (Balilla class)

Dimensions: Length 86.5m (283.8ft), Beam 7.8m (25.7ft), Draught 4.7m (15.4ft)

Displacement (surface/submerged): 1450 tonnes (1427t) / 1904 tonnes/1874t)

Propulsion: two diesels 1827kW (2450hp), two 800kW (1100hp) electric motors, two screws

Speed (surface/submerged): 17.5kt (32.4kmh, 20.1mph) / 8.9kt (16.5kmh, 10.2mph)

Range (surface/submerged): 12,000nm (22,224km, 13,809mi) at 7kt / 110nm (200km, 130mi) at 3kt

Armament: six 533mm (21in) torpedo tubes, 12 torpedoes; one 120mm (4.7in) deck gun, two 13.2mm (0.5in) machine guns

Crew: 77

A *Balilla* class submarines moored at a port somewhere in Italy. From 1934, a second 4.7in/45cal gun was installed in an extension to the tower.

Domenico Millelire

In order to get under anti-submarine nets and avoid entanglement, submarines involved in inshore attacks, or having to pass through narrow protected straits, had a pair of heavy wires rigged from bow to tower and stern (as illustrated here). These were intended to lift the base of the net without the hull being touched.

Enrico Toti

The only Italian submarine to sink a Royal Navy submarine in World War II, *Toti* was already quite elderly on 15 October 1940. It was attached to the 40th Squadron of the 4th Submarine Group at Taranto, making patrols into the Ionian Sea. *Enrico Toti* remained afloat as a harbour pontoon from 1943–46.

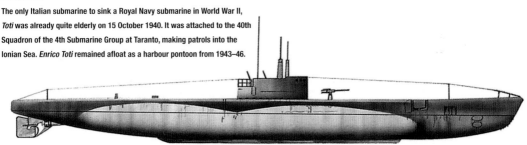

the open deck, these were the largest guns on Italian submarines of the period, intended for use on unarmed ships. *Enrico Tazzoli* was fitted for minelaying, with 14 mines in two stern tubes. The class underwent significant changes in the war years, with *Enrico Tazzoli* and *Giuseppe Finzi* having the long towers shortened and reduced in height. From March 1943, *Tazzoli* and *Finzi* were converted to long-range transport boats.

Enrico Tazzoli

Like the *Balilla* class, which it resembled, the *Calvi* class was designed by the civilian Ansaldo team. With a full double hull, and improved crew facilities, it was meant for long-range work. Prior to conversion as a transport, *Tazzoli* had sunk 96,553 gross registered tonnage (GRT) of Allied shipping in the Atlantic and Mediterranean.

Enrico Tazzoli (Calvi class)

Dimensions: Length 84.3m (276.7ft), Beam 7.7m (25.4ft), Draught 5.2m (17.1ft)

Displacement (surface/submerged): 1549 tonnes (1525t) / 2061 tonnes (2028t)

Propulsion: two 1641kW (2200hp) diesels, two 671kW (2900hp) electric motors, two screws

Speed (surface/submerged): 16.8kt (31.1kmh, 19.3mph) / 7.4kt (13.7kmh, 8.5mph)

Range (surface/submerged): 11,400nm (21,112km, 13,100mi) at 8kt / 120nm (220km, 140mi) at 3kt

Armament: eight 533mm (21in) torpedo tubes, 16 torpedoes; two 120mm (4.7in) deck guns, two twin 13.2mm (0.5in) machine guns

Crew: 77

Squalo and Sirena classes (1928–31)

Some historians consider _Squalo_ to mark the end of Italy's 'experimental' era. However, adaptations continued.

Designed by the Bernardis bureau and built at the CRDA Monfalcone yard, the four-strong _Squalo_ class was single-hulled and in most respects a repeat of the preceding _Bandiera_ class. It still had the bulbous raised bow form, which held an air tank intended to improve surface buoyancy and prevent pitching, and side blisters were added for further stability.

As with many other Italian submarines, the large tower was substantially cut back in 1941–42. Propulsion was by two Fiat diesels of 1100kW (1500hp) and two 485kW (650hp) CRDA electric motors. Of intermediate type in size, its relatively limited range confined it to coastal action.

Sirena Class

Following the London Naval Treaty of 1930, the Sirena class of 12 was the second group after the _Argonauta_ class (1930–32) to conform (up to a point) to the 600-ton rule. All were built between 1931 and 1934, the first six at CRDA, and two each by Tosi, Cantieri Quarnaro (Fiume), and OTO (La Spezia). Construction began before the first of the _Argonauta_ boats had been tested, and differences were

A _Squalo_-class submarine at a naval review, circa 1940. Italian destroyers can be seen in the background.

Delfino

Delfino's wartime cruises amounted to 17,429nm (32,379km, 20,057mi), of which 1756, just over 10 per cent, were submerged.

Delfino (Squalo class)

Dimensions: Length 69.8m (229ft), Beam 7.21m (23.7ft), Draught 5.19m (17ft)

Displacement (surface/submerged): 920 tonnes (905t) / 1125 tonnes (1107t)

Propulsion: two diesels of 1100kW (1500hp), two 485kW (650hp) electric motors, two screws

Speed (surface/submerged): 15.1kt (28kmh, 17.4mph) / 8kt (15kmh, 9.2mph)

Range (surface/submerged): 5650nm (10,464km, 6502mi) at 8kt / 100nm (185km, 115mi) at 3kt

Armament: eight 533mm (21in) torpedo tubes, 12 torpedoes; one 102mm (4in) deck gun, two single 13.2mm (0.5in) machine guns

Crew: 53

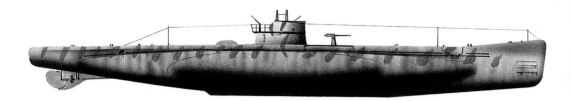

THE '600' TYPE

This designation was used from 1930 for Italy's mid-size submarines, to distinguish them from the larger ocean-cruising boats. It came from the London Naval Treaty of 1930, limiting the size of such craft to 600 tons. Even the first of the submarines that followed, the *Argonauta* class, was closer to 700 tons, and its successors were even larger. In all, there were five of the type: *Argonauta, Sirena, Perla, Adua* and *Acciaio*, with a total of 59 boats. Some Italian naval historians regard them as five series within a single class. Construction of the '600s' followed a standard plan. All were Bernardis type. The cylindrical pressure hull was formed from steel rings set around 520mm (20.5in) apart, to which double overlapping nickel steel plates were riveted (only in the final *Acciaio* class was welding employed). The plates were 15mm (0.59in) thick at midships, thinning to 12mm (0.47in) towards each end. Internally the hull was divided into six zones, separated by watertight bulkheads: forward torpedo room, including petty officers' space; officers' space and forward battery compartment; control room with access to the conning tower and cubicles for radio and hydrophone operation; auxiliary machine room and aft battery hold; diesel engine room; electric motors and aft torpedo room (including crew bunks). The forward torpedo area also held a galley, electric-powered, and a second galley, oil-fired, was in the tower (discontinued in the final *Acciaio* class).

Propulsion on the '600' types was from two-stroke reversible diesel engines produced by Italian factories: CRDA, Fiat and Tosi in either four- or six-cylinder format (mostly the latter). Power output was gradually increased, from 1250hp on *Argonauta* to 1350hp on Sirena and 1400hp on *Perla, Adua* and *Acciaio*. Drive was direct to the propellers, with the use of de-clutching when the batteries were being charged with DC current via the electric motors. These were built by CRDA, *Marelli* and *Ansaldo* and were held in two compartments with 52 batteries in each. Each could be operated independently. Total battery weight was 74 tonnes (72.8t). Compressed air was used to blow the ballast tanks, fire torpedoes, and start up the main engines. The primary compressor, electrically powered, was housed in the auxiliary machine room but 'supercompressors' were built into the diesel engines, usable only when the boat was open to the outer air.

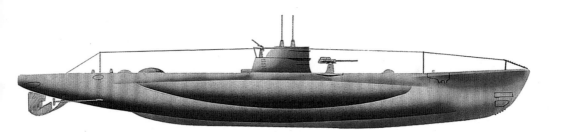

Galatea

International agreements limited the size of coastal submarines to 610 tonnes (600 tons) and the Italians and French both had several '600' designs, though size tended to creep up with successive variants. Most of the *Sirena* class saw intensive action in the Mediterranean in 1940–43, and all except *Galatea* were lost. It was stricken after the war in 1948.

very small. They were single-hulled, with blisters attached both for balance and for additional tankage. The diesel engines were either Fiat or Tosi.

Wartime variations included modifications to the towers and the original AA armament of two 13.2mm guns was increased to four. Some of the class were also equipped with two Breda 6.5mm light machine guns.

Galatea (Sirena class)

Dimensions: Length 60.18m (197.4ft), Beam 6.45m (21.2ft), Draught 4.7m (15.4ft)

Displacement (surface/submerged): 691 tonnes (680t) / 850 tonnes (837t)

Propulsion: two diesels of 505kW (625hp), two 300kW (400hp) electric motors, two screws

Speed (surface/submerged): 14kt (26kmh, 16mph) / 7.5kt (13.9kmh, 8.6mph)

Range (surface/submerged): 5000nm (9260km, 5755mi) at 8kt / 72nm (133km, 83mi) at 4kt

Armament: six 533mm (21in) torpedo tubes, 12 torpedoes; one 100mm (3.9in) deck gun 2–4 single or twin 13.2mm (0.5in) machine guns

Crew: 45

Velella

A good sea-boat, the *Argo*-class *Velella* also saw much action. Though classed as coastal, it was among the submarines sent to Bordeaux for Atlantic service, making four patrols between November 1940 and August 1941. Its sinking in September 1943, while opposing Allied landings at Salerno, was on the day before the Armistice (already signed) was announced.

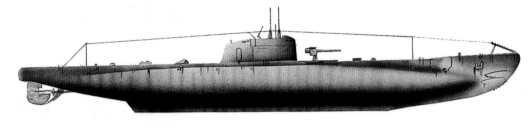

Adua class (1936–38)

The 17 *Adua* boats were constructed and commissioned with rapidity, the class leader laid down in January 1936 and delivered in November of the same year.

All were in service by October 1938, the work shared by the three yards of Monfalcone (CRDA), La Spezia (OTO) and Taranto (Tosi). This reflects confidence in the now-established '600' type design begun with the *Argonauta* class. They were short-range, single-hulled, with midships ballast tanks inside the hull, and side blisters. Minor differences in appearance reflected the different constructors, and the machinery, though of the same power rating, came from each yard's own works or suppliers.

Italian submarines tended to be underpowered compared to German or British boats and consequently slower, though otherwise highly effective attack boats. Like most other classes, most but not all had dismountable T-form deck masts fore and aft to support radio aerial and net-avoidance cables; most sported a serrated, angled bow net-cutter. The towers on most of the class were altered

in 1942–43 to enable retraction of the periscopes and to provide extra AA mounts.

In 1940 *Gondar* and *Scire* were converted to carry SLC-type human torpedoes. The towers were reduced in size, the deck guns were removed and the cylindrical containers, welded to the deck, were pressurized to allow the submarine to go deep (maximum 80m (260ft).

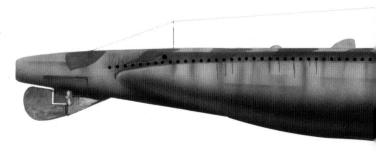

Dagabur

Dimensions: Length 60.28m (197.75ft), Beam 6.45m (21.2ft), Draught 4.64m (15.25ft)

Displacement (surface/submerged): 697.2 tonnes (686t) /856.4 tonnes (843t)

Propulsion: two diesels of 500kW (700hp), two 300kW (400hp) electric motors, two screws

Speed (surface/submerged): 14kt (26kmh, 16mph) / 7.5kt (13.9kmh, 8.6mph)

Range (surface/submerged): 3180nm (5889km, 3659mi) at 10.5kt / 74nm (137km, 85mi) at 4kt

Armament: six 533mm (21in) torpedo tubes, 12 torpedoes; one 100mm (3.9in) deck gun, two 13.2mm (0.5in) machine guns

Crew: 44

TORPEDOES

Italy's main torpedo factories were Whitehead (W) at Fiume (now Rijeka), with a secondary plant, Silurificio Moto Fides near Leghorn; and Silurificio Italiano (SI) at Baia (Naples). Italy entered the war with a stock of both 533 and 450mm torpedoes, and some submarines were fitted with reducing frames in the 533mm tubes to fire the slimmer version. All used the wet-heater type of engine, and there was little difference in performance between the types: Italian torpedoes were recognized as superior to those of other European navies. The Type W 4x7.2 Veloce weighed 1700kg (3784lb), was 7.2m (23.6ft) long, with a 270kg (595lb) explosive charge, and could run for 4000m (4400yd) at 50kt, or 12,000m (13,100yd) at 30kt. SI had a similar model but with a lower speed range of 8000m (8750yd). At the Baia factory, Carlo Calosi devised a magnetic detonator which equipped the torpedo with its own magnetic field, overcoming the problem of sensitivity to the variability of Earth's magnetic field. After Italy's surrender, he assisted the Allies in developing a countermeasure.

Dagabur

Adua-class *Dagabur* had an active career in the Mediterranean until picked up on the Type 271 radar of the destroyer HMS *Wolverine* on the night of 12 August 1942. The submarine, with no surface radar, was rammed and sunk.

Adua

Adua was the lead submarine in its class. Note the revised conning tower in this illustration, dating from 1942.

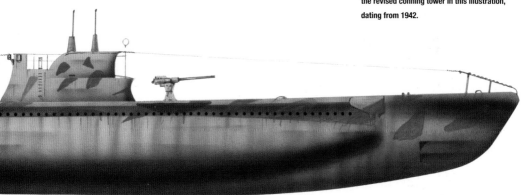

Foca and Marcello classes (1936–38)

The three *Foca*-class boats were fitted as minelayers, though the extent of their activity as such is not clear.

They could set 36 mines, 20 held in a central magazine, released via watertight hatch, and 16 in two stern chutes. Six torpedo tubes, four forward and two stern, were also fitted, but only 6 torpedoes could be carried. The tower was placed unusually far forward to allow for mine storage, and the squared stern was angled downwards to the waterline. The hull was partially double, and the boat could operate down to 90m (300ft).

The 100mm (3.9in) deck gun, originally placed on the tower, facing aft, was moved forward on *Atropo* and *Zoea* in 1941 when the size of the tower was reduced. The class also carried two twin 13.2mm (0.52in) machine guns.

Marcello Class

The eleven Marcellos were long-range single-hull boats, built to a Bernardis design, derived from the *Glauco* class. Blister tanks were fitted. Originally a tall casing was built above the tower for the periscopes,

Marcello class submarine *Angelo Emo* was launched in 1938. *Emo* was sunk by the naval trawler HMS *Lord Nuffield* on 7 November 1942 during the preliminary stages of Operation Torch.

Barbarigo (Marcello class)

Dimensions: Length 73m (239.5ft), Beam 7.19m (23.6ft), Draught 5.1m (16.75ft)

Displacement (surface/submerged): 1080 tonnes (1060t) / 1334 tonnes (1313t)

Propulsion: two diesels of 1342kW (1800bhp), two 410kW (550hp) electric motors, two screws

Speed (surface/submerged): 17.4kt (32.2kmh, 20mph) / 8kt (15kmh, 9.2mph)

Range (surface/submerged): 7500nm (13,890km, 8631mi) at 9.4kt / 8nm (15km, 9.2mi) at 8kt

Armament: eight 533mm (21in) torpedo tubes, 12 torpedoes; two 100mm (3.9in) deck guns, two twin 13.2mm (0.5in) machine guns

Crew: 57

Barbarigo

Barbarigo was one of two *Marcello*-class boats converted in 1943 as a transport craft. To keep reserve buoyancy at a safe level they lost their torpedo tubes, deck gun and attack periscope, allowing for a cargo capacity of 160 tonnes (158 tons).

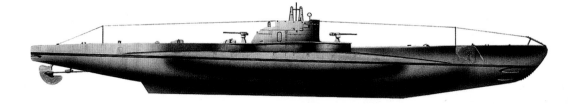

GUNS AND PIGS

The *Balilla* and *Calvi* class boats engaged in the war were fitted with 120mm (4.7in) deck guns. But the standard main gun became the 100mm (3.9in)/47cal type, with various modifications. Older mountings from 1927 were replaced by a 1935 type to give greater elevation. It was a reliable gun, firing eight to 10 rounds a minute, with 13.8kg (30.4lb) HE shells, but not suited to AA defence. Range was 12,800m (13,800yd) at 350. The standard AA gun was the 13.2m (0.52in) Model 31 produced by the Breda company. Based on a French Schneider/Hotchkiss design, M1929, it could be set on a single or double mount. Gas-operated, air-cooled, it was fed from a 30-round magazine. Its effective AA range was 4000m (13,200ft) at 800. Breda also produced a Model 35, but it was little used. Had Italy stayed in combat, heavier AA defences would certainly have been needed.

The manned SLC torpedoes known as *maiale* (pigs) were carried on a number of modified submarines, including most famously Scire of the *Adua* class in the raid on Alexandria harbour of 3 December 1941. In the earliest versions of the project, SLC diversion vehicles were to be hoisted on the deck of the submarine carrier and secured to it with cables. This was soon abandoned, and a special cylindrical container for the transport of 'Pigs' was developed. Such units could be mounted on any suitable submarine and did not affect the diving or the submerged operation of the carrier.

The Perla-class *Ambra* and *Idride* had their 100mm (3.9in) guns removed to make room for containers for torpedoes: three on *Ambra* and four on *Idride*. Two Adua-class submarines were adapted: *Gondar* and *Scire*. *Grongo* and *Murena* (Flutto class), built in 1943, were also earmarked for four containers. However, in early September 1943, these boats were scuttled. Later they were raised, but the *maiale* cradles were not installed.

but this was removed in wartime. and a DF loop aerial was placed behind the bridge. More powerful diesels (CRDA for the first nine, Fiat for two) of 2684kW (3600bhp) gave them a surface speed of up to 18.5kt. Bunker capacity of 60 tonnes (59t) enabled a range of 12,070km (7500mi) at 9.4kt. In wartime the towers went through diverse re-shaping, two with AA platforms resembling the U-boats' winter gardens. The *Marcello* boats were regarded as highly effective and manoeuvrable, with a submerged endurance of 120nm (222km, 138mi) at 3kt. They were also well-armed for surface action with 100mm (3.9in) guns fore and aft. From August 1940, the class operated from Bordeaux, standing up well to Atlantic conditions.

Zoea

Described as coastal boats despite their size, the class was also heavily armed for minelayers. *Foca* was lost off Palestine in October 1940 following the Italian surrender, while *Zoea* and *Atropo* were both integrated into the Allied fleet.

Zoea (Foca class)
Dimensions: Length 82.85m (271.8ft), Beam 7.17m (23.5ft), Draught 5.2m (17.1ft)
Displacement (surface/submerged): 1326 tonnes (1305t) /1651 tonnes (1625t)
Propulsion: two diesels of 1075kW (1440hp), 465kW (2625hp) electric motors, two screws
Speed (surface/submerged): 15.2kt (28.2kmh, 17.5mph) / 7.4kt (13.7kmh, 8.5mph)
Range (surface/submerged): 7800nm (14,446km, 8976mi) at 8kt / 120nm (222km, 138mi) at 4kt
Armament: six 533mm (21in) torpedo tubes, 12 torpedoes; one 100mm (3.9in) deck gun, two twin 13.2mm (0.5in) machine guns
Crew: 60

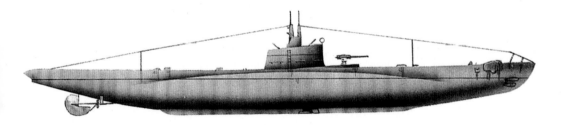

Marconi and Cagni classes (1938–41)

Six-strong, the Marconis were the *Regia Marina*'s most successful class. A wider operating range of 10,500nm (19,446km, 12,083mi) was the main difference between the six *Marconi* class boats and the *Marcellos*.

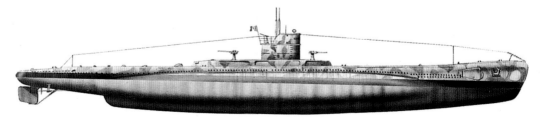

Marconi class

Both were highly effective in action and performed well in the Atlantic. The *Marconi* class were also single-hulled with blister bulges, but slightly narrower and longer. Power came from the same CRDA diesels of a combined 2684.5kW (3600hp) as the Marcellos, but the two *Marelli* electric motors were uprated to a combined 1118.5kW (1500hp). Fuel capacity was 73 tonnes (72t). Operational depth was down to 90m (288ft). The original towers, with a tall narrow periscope casing rising above the oblong base, were cut back in 1941–42, in reaction to Atlantic weather and fighting conditions. Periscope sleeves were also brought lower, as

Ammiraglio Cagni

Built at Monfalcone to a Bernardis design, this boat made some of the longest patrols of any World War II submarine, operating into the South Atlantic for up to 135 days.

on other classes. A warload of 16 torpedoes was carried. They mounted a single 100mm (3.9in) 47cal gun, on the foredeck, and for AA defence two twin 13.2mm (0.5in) guns were mounted in the tower.

In the summer of 1942 *Leonardo da Vinci* was temporarily modified to carry a CA-2 midget submarine on the foredeck, which could be launched underwater. The aim was a stealth attack on New York harbour,

Ammiraglio Cagni (Cagni class)

Dimensions: Length 87.95m (288.5ft), Beam 7.76m (25.5ft), Draught 5.72m (18.8ft)

Displacement (surface/submerged): 1700 tonnes (1653t) / 2190 tonnes (2136t)

Propulsion: two diesels of 1630kW (2185hp); two 650kW (900hp) electric motors; two screws

Speed (surface/submerged): 17kt (31kmh, 19.5mph) / 8.5kt (15.7kmh, 9.8mph)

Range (surface/submerged: 13,500nm (25,002km, 15,536mi) at 9kt / 93nm (172km, 107mi) at 3.5kt

Armament: Fourteen 450mm (17.7in) torpedo tubes, 36 torpedoes; two 100mm (4in) 47cal deck guns, four 13.2mm (1in) AA guns

Crew: 85

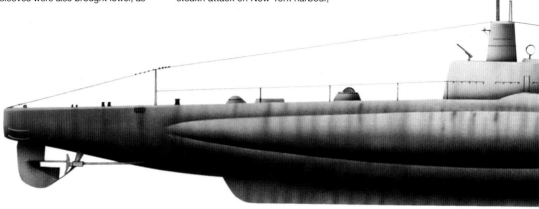

The class leader, *Guglielmo Marconi*, launched at Monfalcone on 27 July 1939. It disappeared in the Atlantic at the end of October 1941.

which was cancelled. The fittings were later removed, and the deck gun was restored. Planned conversion to a transport submarine in 1943 was forestalled by its sinking on 23 May that year.

Cagni class

The Cagni class, the *Regia Marina's* largest attack submarine, was a rather strange vessel to build in 1939–41. It was designed to attack merchant shipping on the high seas, and also to operate as far away as the East African coast. For the first purpose

it was fitted with 14 450mm (17.7in) torpedo tubes, eight in the bow, six at the stern; and 36 torpedoes; for the second it had a fuel capacity of 183 tonnes (180t) and other facilities to allow for up to six months at sea. The tower was the same design as for the *Marcello* class but reduced soon after launching.

The diesel engines and electric motors were CRDA, which built all four of the class (12 more were cancelled). In the event, they were mostly used as transports, and only *Cagni* operated as an ocean cruiser.

Leonardo da Vinci (Marconi class)

Dimensions: Length 76.5m (251ft), Beam 6.81m (22.3ft), Draught 4.72m (15.5ft)

Displacement (surface/submerged): 1194 tonnes (1175t) / 1489 tonnes (1465t)

Propulsion: two diesels of 1342.5kW (1800hp), two 556kW (750hp) electric motors, two screws

Speed (surface/submerged): 17.8kt (33kmh, 20.5mph) / 8.2kt (15.2kmh, 9.4mph)

Range (surface/submerged): 9124nm (16,898km, 10,500mi) at 8kt / 95.6nm (177km, 110mi) at 3kt

Armament: eight 533mm (21in) torpedo tubes, 12 torpedoes; one 100mm (4in) 47cal deck gun, four 13.3mm (0.79in) machine guns

Crew: 57

Leonardo da Vinci

Leonardo da Vinci as fitted for the planned New York attack, with the CA-2 in place of the deck gun. The tall fairing around the periscopes was removed to reduce the boat's silhouette. As with many other submarine classes, the Marconi boats showed tower-shape variations as the war went on.

CB-class midget submarine (1941–43)

Manned torpedoes and midget submarines were important tactical weapons in Italy's naval strategy, both in the Mediterranean and Black seas.

At the start of hostilities, Italy gained experience from the CA class of midget submarines. CB was a much-improved development, 22 in number, intended for penetration of anchorages. Built by the Caproni company in Milan, they had a considerable surface profile compared to the British X-craft, with a fairing built on top of the pressure hull supporting a breakwater and small observation tower, which would certainly have made surface movement easier. On each side of the tower, a 457mm (18in) loaded torpedo tube was mounted, its weapon fired by compressed air. Internally there were two compartments: navigation centre and engine room, separated by a light bulkhead. Two Calzoni pumps were mounted forward for diving and surfacing. The boat was driven and powered by an Isotta-Fraschini 67kW (90hp) diesel engine and a 37kW (50hp) Brown Boveri electric motor. Batteries were placed below the navigation room.

Equipment

The boats were fitted with gyrocompass, magnetic compass, radio gear, and periscope. A hydrophone set was mounted in a frame at the fore-end of the keel. Maximum operational depth was 55m (180ft).

Opposite & below: A CB-class midget submarine docked at Taranto, Italy, following the surrender of the Italian fleet to the Allies, November 1943. The torpedo tubes can clearly be seen fixed to the side of the boat.

CB-12

These were built far inland, in Milan by Caproni Toliedo, but could be moved on special rail trucks. The torpedoes were mounted in external collars. Maximum diving depth was 55m (180ft), and they were equipped to carry 10 man-days of provisions. They were of very similar dimensions to the British X-boats, and, though still slow-speed, were slightly faster. CB-20 is preserved in the Technical Museum, Zagreb.

CB-12

Dimensions (length/beam/draught): 15m (49.4ft) / 3m (9.8ft) / 2.05m (6.75ft)
Displacement (surface/submerged): 36 tonnes (35.4t) / 45 tonnes (44.3t)
Propulsion: one diesel, 67kW (90hp), one 37kW (50hp) electric motor, one screw
Speed (surface/submerged): 7.5kt (13.9kmh, 8.6mph) / 7kt (13kmh, 8.1mph)
Range (surface/submerged): 1216nm (2252km, 1400mi) at 5kt / 43.4nm (80km, 50mi) at 3kt
Armament: two 457mm (18in) torpedo tubes, two torpedoes or two mines
Crew: four

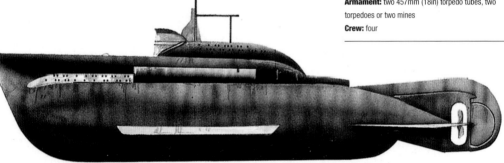

R-class (1942–43)

Only two were completed of what was intended to be a class of 12 large transport submarines, capable of moving high-value cargo between Italy and Japan.

While several older types were converted for this traffic, the R-class was purpose-designed as a cargo vessel, able to hold a load of 610 tonnes (600t). This load was distributed across four holding areas, to maintain balance. Total cargo space was 600m³ (785yd³) – twice the capacity of the German Class XB converted minelayers. They were partially double-hulled, with the holds having the same pressure resistance as the pressure hull, with a testing depth of 100m (330ft). Each hold was accessed by a collapsible deck-mounted crane. The towers were low to minimize surface visibility. Propulsion was from two Tosi diesels of a combined 1938kW (2600hp) and two Marelli motors of 671kW (900hp). With a surfaced range of 12,000nm (22,224km, 13,809mi), they had storage for 203 tonnes (200t)

of fuel, but their speed was relatively slow. Operating depth was down to 80m (260ft).

Non-combat boats

The first two, *Romolo* and *Remo*, were built by Tosi at Taranto and put into service with minimal trials and work-up. The class had no torpedoes and carried three 20mm (0.79in) light AA guns on retractable mounts. The crew was large for a non-fighting ship, but the class, designed for long endurance, had better habitation and stores facilities than combat boats.

After *Remo* and *Romolo* had been laid down, it was decided to equip the class with two 450mm (17.7in) torpedo tubes. But these were not fitted to the two boats actually commissioned. Both boats were sunk by Allied attack before they could even be loaded up.

Remo **(R-class)**
Dimensions: Length 86.5m (283.8ft), Beam 7.86m (25.75ft), Draught 5.34m (17.5ft)
Displacement (surface/submerged): 2155 tonnes (2121t) / 2560 tonnes (2520t)
Propulsion: two diesels of 950kW (1300bhp), two 335kW (450hp) electric motors, two screws
Speed (surface/submerged): 13kt (24kmh, 15mph) / 6kt (11kmh, 6.9mph)
Range (surface/submerged): 12,000nm (22,224km, 13,809mi) at 9kt / 100nm (190km, 120mi) at 3.5kt
Armament: three 20mm (0.79in) AA guns
Crew: 63

SINGLE OR DOUBLE HULL?

Cavallini and Bernardis, Italy's leading submarine designers, differed on this question. Cavallini preferred the double hull, as developed by Laurenti while Bernardis opted for single-hull designs. Both approaches had their merits, and Bernardis used blisters welded to the hull both for stability and for extra fuel storage. Cavallini was associated with the Tosi shipyard at Taranto, and many of his designs were built there. Bernardis worked primarily with the Adriatic Cantieri Uniti dell'Adriatico at Monfalcone. But larger classes were built in several yards to the same basic design.

Remo

The large hull extended over four watertight holds. *Remo* was torpedoed while on the surface; *Romolo* was also sunk three days later. None of the other boats in the class were completed, though two, R-11 and R-12, were scuttled, refloated and used as oil storage hulks after the war.

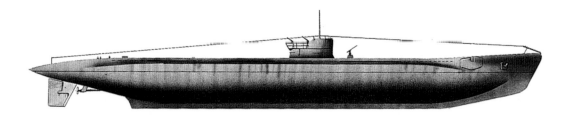

Flutto class (1943)

Italy's surrender in 1943 cut short the development of the *Regia Marina's* final class of submarines.

Following the Bernardis tradition of a partial double hull, the class (sometimes referred to as the *Tritone* class) was conceived as a three-stage programme to allow for corrections and innovations. However, only 10, from the first series, were completed and saw action. The aim was a medium-sized versatile boat that could be built quickly at a reasonable cost, using welding and other rapid-construction techniques. The tower resembled that of a U-boat rather than previous Italian classes, with a railed platform for two twin 13.2mm AA guns.

The periscopes were completely recessed, and it had no second galley. The forward 100mm (3.9in) gun was mounted on a railed platform which overlapped the deck sides.

Powerplant

Power came from two Fiat MEX 328R eight-cylinder diesels of 1790kW (2400hp) and two Marelli motors of 596kW (800hp). 52.8 tonnes (52t) of fuel oil was carried. Two battery sets each of 52 cells were in forward and aft locations, with a total weight of 78 tonnes (76.75t). Operational depth was down to 120m (400ft) with a crash-dive time of 30 seconds. They had six torpedo tubes, four forward and two aft, with six reserve torpedoes.

Of the ten operational boats, six were built by Tosi and four by CRDA. Four of the class were scuttled on Italy's surrender in September 1943 but were raised and used by the Germans as UIT-15,16,19 and 20. They included *Murena*, one of two that had been fitted with containers for carrying *Maiale* manned torpedoes.

Flutto

Dimensions: Length 63.15m (207.2ft), Beam 6.98m (22.9ft), Draught 4.87m (16ft)

Displacement (surface/submerged): 945 tonnes (930t) / 1111 tonnes (1093t)

Propulsion: two diesels of 895kW (1200hp), two 298kW (400hp) electric motors; two screws

Speed (surface/submerged): 16kt (30kmh, 18mph) / 8kt (15kmh, 9mph)

Range (surface/submerged): 5400nm (10,001km, 6214mi) at 8kt / 80nm (150km, 92mi) at 4kt

Armament: six 533mm (21in) torpedo tubes, 12 torpedoes; one 100mm (4in) 47cal deck gun; four 13.2mm (0.5in) machine guns

Crew: 49

Flutto

Completed in March 1943, *Flutto* was one of only three of its class to be engaged in action; all were lost. Two were fitted with cylinders for manned torpedoes, set alongside the tower and not replacing the gun as happened with the Adua class. After the war, *Nautilo* was passed to the Yugoslav Navy, and *Marea* to the Soviets.

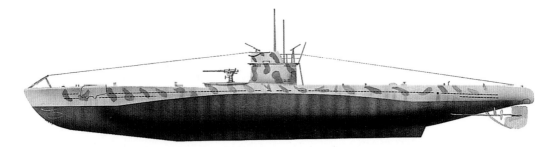

Type C-1 (1937–42)

As with other navies, Japanese design was incremental, with successive classes building on the experience and performance of their predecessors.

Type C-1

Type C-1 24 was part of the Pearl Harbor attack fleet. The deck gun was moved forward of the tower when midget subs rather than aircraft were to be carried.

Changes often related to intended function. The five C-1 class, double-hulled, numbered I-16, 18, 20, 22 and 24, did not carry an aircraft: instead, they were fitted with cradles to hold midget submarines (A Type) and carried support equipment. In 1943 I-16 and perhaps the others were adapted to hold two tracked Daihatsu landing craft for supplying island garrisons.

The eight torpedo tubes were all forward, in two torpedo rooms, one above the other. Twenty torpedoes were carried. A 140mm (5.5in)/50cal deck gun and two Type 96 25mm (1in) AA guns were fitted.

Powerplant

Powerful machinery, two Kampon Mk2 Model 10 diesel engines of 6200hp each and two electric motors of 1000hp each, enabled a surface speed of 23.5kt and 8kt submerged. Maximum operating depth was 100m (330ft).

The C-type was developed into the Type C Modified (three boats) and the projected V-22B.

Type C-1

Dimensions: Length 109.3m (358.6ft), Beam 9.1m (29.8ft), Draught 7.8m (25.7ft)

Displacement (surface/submerged): 2219 tonnes (2184t) / 3618 tonnes (3561t)

Propulsion: two diesels of 4623kW (6200bhp), two 745kW (1000hp) electric motors, two screws

Speed (surface/submerged): 23.6kt (43.7kmh, 27mph) / 8kt (14.8kmh, 9.2mph)

Range (surface/submerged): 14,000nm (25,928km, 16,111mi) at 16kt / 60nm (110km, 69mi) at 3kt

Armament: eight 533mm (21in) torpedo tubes, 20 torpedoes; one 140mm (5.5in) deck gun; two Type 96 25mm (1in) AA guns

Crew: 95

JAPANESE IDENTIFIERS

The designations I, Ro, and Ha of submarine types began as generic, denoting ocean-going, medium-range/coastal, and small or midget submarines respectively, each including a range of types. Individual classes and types have their own identifiers, either a combination of letters and numbers, as K6, or simply a number, as in I-201. From May 1942, all submarine types were given the prefix number 1. For example, K6 became K16.

Commissioned in April 1944, I-55 was lost in July 1944 while taking part in the Marianas campaign aftern being depth-charged by US destroyers.

'Type A' midget submarine Ha-19 sits aground on an eastern Oahu beach, following attempts to enter Pearl Harbor during the 7 December 1941 Japanese attack. The photograph was taken shortly after 8 December 1941.

Type C-1

Dimensions: Length 23.9m (78.6ft), Beam 1.8m (5.11t), Draught 3m (9.10ft)

Displacement (submerged): 47 tonnes (46t)

Propulsion: one electric motor, 447kW (600hp) at 1800rpm

Speed (surface/submerged): 23 knots (43km/h; 26mph); 19 knots (35km/h; 22mph)

Range (surface/submerged): 100nmi (190km) at 2kn (3.7km/h; 2.3mph)

Armament: two 450mm (17.7in) torpedoes, muzzle-loaded into tube

Crew: 2

Type B-1 (1938–43)

The Type B-1 was the Imperial Japanese Navy's most numerous class of ocean-going submarines.

Also known as the I-15 class, these submarines integrated the roles of scouting craft for a battle fleet and attack boats. Double-hulled, more attention was paid to streamlining than in preceding classes. Diesels of 9246kW (12,400bhp) gave a surface speed of 23.5kt. A Yokosuka E14Y reconnaissance aircraft was carried in a faired hangar, launched from a pneumatic catapult on the long foredeck, and retrieved with a collapsible crane (one boat, I-17 had the hangar and catapult facing aft).

Modification

From 1941, the aircraft was removed from some, either to mount a second 140mm (5.5in) gun or (I-36 and I-37 in late 1944) to carry *Kaiten* manned torpedoes. Operating depth was down to 100m (330ft). Despite their size, the IJN boats had poor habitability for their large crews, though still perhaps better than German and British submarines offered.

JAPANESE SNORKELS

In October 1943 the submarine I-8 brought from Germany, amongst other vital cargo, full details of the German snorkel equipment. It took some time for the Navy and industry to develop their own version, which was seen as more useful for charging the batteries than for low-speed movement underwater and was also difficult to adapt to the two-stroke main engines of most Japanese submarines. The design, with wide downwards-turned intake and exhaust tubes, was quite bulky and could not be operated in the relatively unobtrusive manner of Allied versions.

Type B-1

Dimensions: Length 108.7m (356.7ft), Beam 9.3m (30.5ft), Draught 5.1m (16.75in)

Displacement (surface/submerged): 2631 tonnes (2589t) / 3713 tonnes (3654t)

Propulsion: two diesels of 4600kW (6200hp), two 750kW (1000hp) electric motors, two screws

Speed (surface/submerged): 23.5kt (43.5kmh, 27mph) / 8kt (15kmh, 9.2mph)

Range (surface/submerged): 14,000nm (25,928km, 16,111mi) at 16kt / 96nm (178km, 110mi) at 3kt

Armament: six torpedo tubes, 17 torpedoes; one 140mm (5in) 50cal deck gun, two 25mm (1in) AA guns

Crew: 101

I-15

In the Guadalcanal battles of August 1942, the Japanese deployed the big submarines in a screen in advance of the fleet, with the senior officer in a command boat. Co-ordination was difficult, but either I-15 or I-19 hit the battleship *North Carolina* with a torpedo and I-15 narrowly missed USS *Washington*.

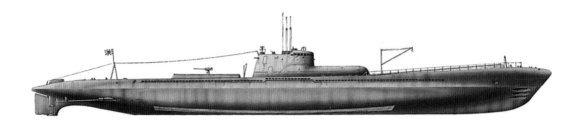

Type KD7 (1940–43)

The line of KD *(Kaidai)* submarines began in 1925 with KD1. All Kaidai-class submarines originally had a two-digit boat name, from I-51 onwards.

The KD-7 (I-176 class) of ten boats was the final specification, and unlike its immediate predecessors, had only medium-range endurance, though still classed as an ocean-going attack boat. It did not handle well when submerged and after 1942 three were converted to transports, for which their high surface speed was well-suited. Propulsion was by two-stroke Kampon Mk 1B Model 8 diesels giving 5966kW (8000shp) As transports they normally carried a small landing craft to ferry supplies ashore. The six torpedo tubes were all forward-facing.

KD7

Dimensions (length/beam/draught): 105.5m (346.2in) / 8.25m (27.1ft) / 4.6m (15.1ft)

Displacement (surface/submerged): 1656 tonnes (1630t) / 2644 tonnes / 2602t

Propulsion: two diesels of 2983kW (4000hp), two 671kW (900hp) electric motors, two screws

Speed (surface/submerged): 23.1kt (42.8kmh, 26.6mph) / 8kt (14.8kmh, 9.2mph)

Range (surface/submerged): 8000nm (14,816km, 9206mi) at 16kt / 50nm (93km, 107mi) at 5kt

Armament: six 533mm (21in) torpedo tubes, 12 torpedoes; one 120mm (4.7in) L/40 deck gun, two Type 96 25mm (1in) AA guns

Crew: 86

I-7

This was an expanded version of the KD-6 patrol submarine design. The intended scouting role of I-7 and I-8 was heavily curtailed by American use of carrier-borne attack planes, though both were refitted with extra AA guns in 1942. They were not well adapted to attack mode despite being fast on the surface. Destroyers were faster.

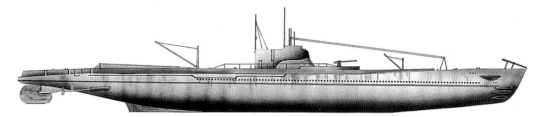

I-73

I-73 of Type KD6A, was torpedoed on the surface and sunk by USS *Gudgeon* (SS211) on 27 January 1942.

Type KS Ro 100 (1941–44)

Japanese strategists fatally underestimated the speed and ferocity with which the USA would take the Pacific War right to the Japanese homeland.

This class of 18 boats, comparatively small but still double-hulled, was planned for coastal and island defence, with four torpedo tubes and carrying only 8 torpedoes and one 76mm (3in) AA gun. Its diving limit was 74m (254ft). Despite excellent underwater manoeuvrability, they were swept away by well-honed ASW methods from destroyers and aircraft. Many of the class had a single 76mm (3in) 40cal gun instead of 2 Type 96 AA guns.

JAPANESE RADAR AND DETECTION SYSTEMS

Japan had used hydrophones in underwater detection since 1930. The Type 93 Model 1 system had a range of 9000m (9840yd). It used 16 receivers set in two elliptical arrays on each side of the vessel's keel. More sophisticated was the Model 2, in use from 1942, with a range up to 6000m (6560yd). From late 1944 there was also Type 3 Model 1, active sonar using the German technology of the *Sondergerät*.

Japanese radar systems lagged behind American and British practice in sophistication and reliability. Radar was fitted on submarines only from April 1944. This was a Type 13 air search, with a 97km (60mi) range for detection of air groups, and 48km (30mi) for a single aircraft. It had a dipole antenna array with mat reflector. For surface search Type 22 was carried, with a range of 34km (21mi). It had a distinctive horn-type antenna. For passive radar detection, the Type E27/3 was used.

Submarine crew

An interior shot of an I-400 hangar, with the Japanese crew preparing to leave after the vessel's surrender, August 1945.

Ro 100

Dimensions: Length 60.9m (199.8ft), Beam 6m (19.7ft), Draught 3.51m (11.5ft)

Displacement (surface/submerged): 611 tonnes (601t) / 795 tonnes (782t)

Propulsion: two diesels of 375kW (500hp), two 285kW (380hp) electric motors, two screws

Speed (surface/submerged): 14.2kt (26.3kmh, 16.3mph) / 8kt (15kmh, 9.2mph)

Range (surface/submerged): 3500nm (6482km, 4028mi) at 12kt / 60nm (110km, 69mi) at 3kt

Armament: four 533mm (21in) torpedo tubes; four Type 96 25mm (1in) AA guns

Crew: 38

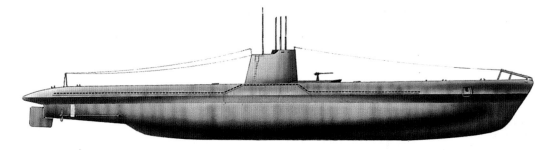

Type I-400 (1943–45)

In 1942, under the Fifth Fleet Replenishment Programme, a total of 18 super-submarines, designated *Sen-Toku* (special class), were included.

Work commenced immediately, and I-400 was laid down at Kure on 18 January 1943. Only two were commissioned into service, in early 1945. Special sea-air missions were intended, including an attempt to block the Panama Canal (the USN's most vital artery). A single pressure hull could not have provided sufficient space, and the unique design was based on a pair of parallel linked cylindrical pressure hulls inside an outer hull. The tower was above the port hull, with the control centre below. The hangar was mounted on the centreline, opening to a 26m (85.3ft) compressed air catapult set in the forward deck at a slight upward angle. A 4.6 tonne (4.5t) collapsible retrieval crane was on the port side. Three planes could be carried, plus parts for a fourth.

Two diesel engines were mounted in each hull, with a single electric motor. Direct drive was employed, with two

One of the two surrendered I-400s arriving in Tokyo Bay, manned by a US Navy prize crew, 30 August 1945.

sets of Vulcan hydraulic clutches. Despite the consumption needs of four engines, the I-400 could carry enough fuel to cruise for 37,000nm (68,524km, 42,579mi) at 14kt, and maintain a patrol for 90 days (capacities never fully tested: the vessel had no air conditioning and no flushing toilets). Surface speed could reach 18.75kt but the bulky hull's submerged speed was only 6.5kt. Operational depth was 100m (330ft), less than the boat's own length. The best diving time was 58 seconds, almost twice that of a US *Balao* class boat.

Apart from the eight torpedo tubes (all forward, with 12 reloads), the I-400s mounted a 140mm (5.5in) deck gun and 10 25mm (1in) AA cannon in three twin and one single mounts. The aircraft were Aichi M-6A1 Seiran monoplanes, specially designed for the I-400 class, armed with a single 850kg (1870lb) torpedo or the same weight of bombs.

Type 22 surface search and Type 13 air search radar were fitted, on a telescopic mast on the tower. The boat was given a coating of anechoic material formed from gum, asbestos and adhesive, to reduce its detectability, and also fitted with demagnetizing cables. A snorkel of fixed rather than retractable type was installed during a refit in May 1945. Day and night periscopes of German design were included along with a telescopic radar mast on the tower. At times a dummy funnel was placed behind the

Opposite: I-400 and I-401 alongside the submarine tender USS *Proteus*, 31 August 1945, following the surrender of all Japanese forces.

I-400

Dimensions: Length 122m (400ft), Beam 12m (39.4ft), Draught 7m (23ft)
Displacement (surface/submerged): 5307 tonnes (5223t) / 6760 tonnes (6560t)
Propulsion: four diesels of 1680kW (2250hp), two 1600kW (2100hp) electric motors, two screws
Speed (surface/submerged): 18.7kt (34.6kmh, 21.5mph) / 6.5kt (12kmh, 7.5mph)
Range (surface/submerged): 37,000nm (68,524km, 42,579mi) at 14kt / 60nm (111km, 69mi) at 3kt
Armament: eight 533mm (21in) torpedo tubes, 12 torpedoes; one Type 11 140mm (5.5in) gun; three waterproofed Type 96 triple and one single AA guns
Crew: 157 including aircrew

Type I-400

Profile and plan of the I-400 class. It struck awe into American observers in 1945, but the Japanese war effort would have been better served by more conventional submarines in greater numbers.

Crew quarters
Accommodation was situated towards the stern.

SUBMARINE-BORNE AIRCRAFT

The standard reconnaissance plane was the Yokosuka E14Y, which could also be fitted to drop two 78kg (168lb) bombs. With a two-man crew, its maximum take-off weight was 1600kg (3527lb). Its range was 881km (547mi) and it had a rear-firing Type 92 7.7mm (0.303in) machine gun. The planes carried by the I-400 class were Aichi M6A Seiran ('clear sky storm'). Also, with a two-man crew, they had a maximum take-off weight of 4445kg (9800lb) when loaded with a torpedo or bomb. A single Type 2 13mm (0.5in) machine gun could be worked from the cabin. Their range was 1188km (738mi).

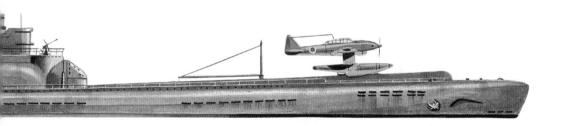

Launching attack floatplane
The key assembly points of the aircraft were marked with fluorescent paint so that they could be assembled in darkness.

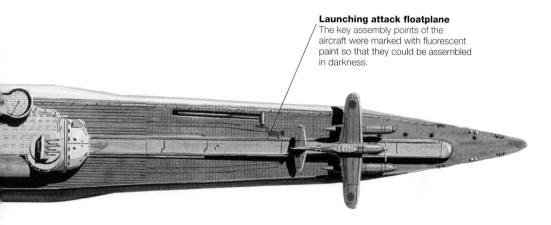

I-400 (*Sentoku* type)

This illustration shows the main features
of Japan's over-ambitious giant.

Deck layout
The upper section with the bridge
deck was canted out on the port side,
with the pressurized conning tower
alongside. The AA placings were to
starboard and port of the centreline.

Kitchen galley
The galley was in the starboard
hull, fitted with giant steam
kettles for preparing rice for the
157-strong crew.

I-400
Great ingenuity went into the folding and collapsible equipment, including a retrieval crane. The three
I-400s were fitted with Mk3 Model 1 air search radar, Mk2 Model 2 surface search radar, and an E 27 radar
detector. I-400 had a German snorkel system from May 1945. All were sunk as targets in 1946.

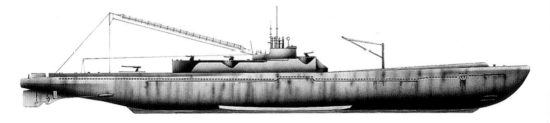

Floatplane
This I-400 mounts a Aichi M6A1 'Seiran' floatplane. The Seirans were launched from a 26m (85ft) Type 4 No. 2 Model 10 compressed-air catapult, rising at a shallow angle from the hangar door.

Crane boom
The crane was capable of lifting approximately 4.6 tonnes (4.5 tons). It was raised mechanically to a height of 8m (26ft) and operated by a motor inside the boat. The boom extended out to a length of 11.8m (39ft).

Hanger
The hangar was 30.48m (100ft) long and 3.34m (11ft wide), its waterproof door secured by a 5mm (2in) rubber gasket.

KAITEN MK1 (1944)

At the other end of the size scale was the Kaiten Mk 1 'human torpedo' of 1944, 15.8m (55ft) long, with a warhead of 1542kg (3400lb). Detonation meant the death of its 'pilot', and 96 personnel were killed in combat or training.

Type I-201 (1943–45)

A late arrival into the Pacific War, the powerful Type 201 was Japan's belated hope to stem the US seaborne onslaught.

As the American war effort in the Pacific intensified through 1943, the IJN command had to accept that its existing submarines were simply incapable of defending themselves against the range of ASW detections and weaponry being deployed against them. Although Japan had built a small experimental high-speed submarine in 1938, this had not been followed up and the boat had been scrapped in 1940. It was not until October 1943 that the formal request was made for an attack submarine that would have high submerged speed and silent running.

Using the 1938 design as a basis, planning was rapid and the first of the new *Sen-Taka* class, I-201, was laid down at Kure Naval Arsenal in March 1944, launched in July and commissioned after trials in February 1945. Only two more were completed.

Hull construction

Electric welding was used as much as possible in the hull construction, with the complete hull assembled from prefabricated sections transported to the launch slip. It was essentially a single-hull design, with the pressure hull occupying 59.2m (194ft) between the bow and stern sections. The tower was small and streamlined, with a narrow upper section supporting the various tubes. The beam was unusually narrow for the boat's length, with retractable forward dive planes in order to reduce underwater resistance, though low-set broad horizontal stern fins increased it to 9.2m (30ft). The hydrophone compartment was set in the keel, well back from the bow.

In the planning and formulation of this design, there is some evidence of cooperation and exchange of information between Japan and Germany, and it is probable that some elements of the late German designs were incorporated in I-201.

Propulsion was provided by two lightweight *Ma-Shiki-Igo* diesels (from a German MAN design), with *Büchi*-type superchargers. Vulcan-type clutches linked them to the propeller shafts. Four electric motors, two in tandem on each shaft and linked by a tail clutch, developed 3728.5kW (5000shp) for submerged power.

The battery sets were each of 2086 cells, the resultant power making the I-201 twice as fast as the US *Balao* class underwater. The designed speed was 15kt on the surface and 20kt submerged. On trials, however, 19kt was the maximum obtained. Full

I-201

Dimensions: Length 79m (259ft), Beam 5.8m (19ft), Draught 7m (23ft)

Displacement (surface/submerged): 1312 tonnes (1291t) / 1470 tonnes (1450t)

Propulsion: two diesels of 1025kW (1375hp), four 932kW (1250hp) electric motors, two screws

Speed (surface/submerged): 15.75kt (29.2kmh, 18mph) / 19kt (35kmh, 21.8mph)

Range (surface/submerged): 15,000nm (27,780km, 17,262mi) at 6kt / 135nm (250km, 155.4mi) at 3kt or 17nm (31km, 19.5 mi) at 19kt

Armament: four 533mm (21in) torpedo tubes, 10 torpedoes; two Type 96 25mm (1in) AA guns

Crew: 50

I-201

I-201 was completed on 2 February 1945 and assigned to various subdivisions of the 6th Fleet. An anechoic rubberized coating was applied to reduce noise. The bow planes were retractable. Ten Type 95 torpedoes were carried. The conning tower is notably small. It was sunk as a target on 23 May 1946.

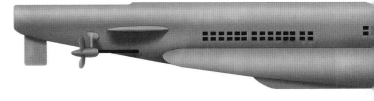

underwater speed could be maintained for a period of 55 minutes, after which the submarine was capable of further movement for twelve hours at 3kt. The maximum operating depth was set at 110m (360ft).

As with previous IJN classes, the four torpedo tubes were all in the bow, with six reloads. The two deck-mounted 25mm Type 96 AA guns, forward and aft of the tower, were retractable to reduce underwater resistance.

Three boats

Only three were launched, but development work went on to the end, focusing particularly on battery capacity. The hulls were given a rubber-based coating to reduce sonar detectability. Wide triangular stabilizer fins were fitted slightly forward of the propellers.

The boats were fitted with snorkels, using a hinged tube set in a slot in the deck. Day and night periscopes of German design were fitted, along with a telescopic radar mast on the tower, all retractable. Unsurprisingly as a new design built in a hurry, I-201 seems to have suffered from a few problems, though these were not apparent until after the Japanese surrender. Designed for a crew of 37, it actually needed 50 men to work it.

A Type I-201 in the Kure area, Japan, late 1945.

Sh (Sen-Ho) Type I-351 (1944–45)

This was a one-boat class, though six were planned. Built at the Kure navy yard, this very large submarine was designed to carry supplies to isolated air bases.

It would hold 390 tonnes (384t) of fuel, ammunition and water. Before completion, it was decided to refit it as an aviation fuel tanker with a capacity of 500,000l (approx. 480 tonnes/472t). The oil was held in the ballast tanks, to be replaced with seawater on the return journey. It was equipped for defence with four 533mm (21in) torpedo tubes, two twin 76mm (3in) trench mortars (naval deck guns not available), one triple and two twin 25mm (1in) AA gun mountings. In addition to its crew, it could accommodate 13 airmen. Fitted with a snorkel, it could spend up to 60 days at sea, and operate to a depth of 90m (300ft).

I-351

Dimensions: Length 111m (364.2ft), Beam 10.2m (33.5ft), Draught 6.1m (20ft)

Displacement (surface/submerged): 3568 tonnes (3512t) / 4359 tonnes (4290t)

Propulsion: two diesels of 1379kW (1850hp); two 445kW (600hp) electric motors, two screws

Speed (surface/submerged): 15.75kt (29.17kmh, 18.1mph) / 6.3kt (11.7kmh, 7.2mph)

Range: 13,000nm (24,076km, 14,960mi) at 14kt / 100nm (190km, 120mi) at 3kt

Armament: four torpedo tubes, four torpedoes; two twin 76mm (3in) mortars; one triple, two twin 25mm (1in) AA guns

Crew: 77

JAPANESE TORPEDOES

IJN submarines were armed with Type 92 and 95 torpedoes, both of 533mm (21in) diameter and 7.1m (23.4ft) length. Type 92 weighed 1724kg (3792lb) with a warhead of 300kg (661lb) and a range of 7000m (7655yd) at 30kt. Type 95 was slightly lighter at 1668kg (3671lb) but with an explosive charge of 406kg (893lb) and a range of 9000m (9842yd) at 49kt and 12,000m (13,123yd) at 45kt. The wakeless Type 95 was the fastest torpedo in common use by any navy during World War II. Its warhead size was the largest of any submarine torpedo, and second only to the Type 93 used by Japanese surface ships. Its engine was a wet-heater type powered by a kerosene/oxygen mix.

The bridge of an I-351 submarine in 1945. The 25mm (1in) AA guns dominate this image of the tower, with the various aerials behind.

I-351

I-351 was sunk by USS *Bluefish* returning from its second voyage to Singapore, on 14 July 1945.

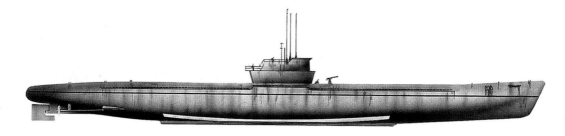

Type Ha 201 (1945)

This *Sensui-taka shoo* (small fast submarine) class was intended to play a big part in coastal defence.

The class was fitted with similar innovations to the larger I-201 type. Despite the modest dimensions they were double-hulled, with a streamlined external casing. The aim was to maximize underwater speed, with minimal equipment or protrusions on the flat upper deck to create drag. A slender tower sat aft of the centre-point. The experimental boat, No. 71, built in 1938, was again taken as a starting point. It had incorporated some advanced features, including a ducted cruciform propeller, not used on the Ha-201 class, though the positioning, set well back from the steering gear, was followed, and X-form control surfaces were used, as were diving planes (not retractable) set aft of the midpoint, as was the tower.

The Ha 201 was to be constructed from prefabricated sections moved to the shipyards for welding together. Shortage of materials and sustained Allied bombing of industrial districts made work very difficult for the builders. But it was a very effective design, able to crash-dive in 15 seconds, with an operating depth of 100m (330ft),

and fitted with a snorkel, enabling it to operate at periscope depth, including attack mode. It was driven by a lightweight intermediate 298kW (400bhp) diesel engine and a 932kW (1250bhp) electric motor and was equipped for 15-day endurance.

The lead boat was laid down at Sasebo Navy Yard on March 1, 1945, and completed on 31 May. By July it was commissioned into the IJN – a timespan that demonstrates the desperate urgency of the situation. With two tubes and two reload torpedoes, the type had limited attack potential, and only a single 7.7mm (0.303in) machine gun on the bridge deck to fend off likely heavy air attacks.

Only large numbers could have made this class a strategic defensive arm. Though 79 were ordered, no more than nine were completed, and none went on war patrol. At the same time, the IJN was building the similar but much slower *Sen-yu-sho* small supply submarines, indicative of a shift towards smaller and more rapidly built boats, again to maximize inshore defence.

Ha 201

Dimensions: Length 53m (173.9ft), Beam 4m (13.1ft), Draught 3.4m (11.25ft)
Displacement (surface/submerged): 325 tonnes (320t) / 447 tonnes (440t)
Propulsion: Intermediate diesel of 298kW (400hp); single 932kW (1250hp) electric motor, single screw
Speed (surface/submerged): 11.8kt (21.9kmh, 13.6mph) / 13.9nm (25.7kmh, 16mph)
Range (surface/submerged): 3000nm (5556km, 3452mi) / 105nm (194km, 121mi) at 2kt
Armament: two 533mm (21in) torpedo tubes, four torpedoes; 17.7mm (0.303in) machine gun
Crew: 26

Ha 201

Underwater speed and precise firepower were the leading characteristics of this class, too late and too few to prove its worth in action.

PART 2: THE ALLIES

Despite having tried to ban armed submarines completely, Britain's Royal Navy applied itself seriously to their development and purpose through the 1920s and 1930s. Its thinking initially was on how submarines could aid in the maintenance of order and protection in the many territories around the world that lived under the Union flag. This did not go away in the 1930s but was compounded by the more immediate threats posed by a resurgent and hostile Germany.

In the USA, the perceived need was to counter the challenge posed by Japan, which required ocean-going submarines, able to operate with surface ships at fleet speed.

In both countries intensive work had been going on since the 1920s to improve the fighting efficiency of submarines. ASDIC detection had been developed in Britain in the course of World War I and was kept secret. Improvements to the somewhat rough-and-ready methods of fire control were pursued, often by individual submariners as well as Navy technicians. The use of radio was expanding, with methods of detection and location as well as communication.

HMS *United* (P44) was a U-class boat commissioned in April 1942.
The deck-mounted D/F and 291W air warning radar antenna are notable.

73

France had its Atlantic and Mediterranean coasts, with rather different conditions, to protect, as well as overseas possessions. Eventually, it abandoned the notion of very large cruiser submarines and opted, like Britain, for mid-size boats that were more adaptable to different requirements, even though this involved compromises in capability. France's capitulation in 1940 opened its naval bases to Germany and Italy but several submarines continued to fight under the Free French flag.

Russian naval ships were effectively bottled up in the Baltic Sea, though submarines operated in the Black Sea. It should also be noted that after the invasion of the Netherlands in May 1940, 18 Dutch submarines continued in action in the Far East. One Polish submarine (Orzel) served with the Royal Navy, and one Yugoslav boat (Nebojsa) was used for training at Alexandria.

The following types are included in this chapter:

FRANCE
● '1500' Type
● '600' and '630' classes
● Surcouf

UNITED KINGDOM
● Oberon and Odin class
● HMS *Porpoise* and Grampus class
● River class
● S-class
● T-class
● U-class
● V-class
● X-class midget submarines

POLAND
● Orzel

SOVIET UNION
● Leninets class
● Shch class

UNITED STATES
● V-boats
● Salmon class
● Gato class
● Balao class
● Tench class

USS *Finback* (SS-230) is launched at Portsmouth Navy Yard, New Hampshire, on 25th August 1941.

'1500' Type (1924–43)

From 1928 right into the war years, France's main class of ocean-going submarines was the '1500-tonne' type.

The lead boat was the *Redoutable*, laid down in August 1924, launched on 1 July 1925, and commissioned on 24 February 1928. The design team, headed by Jean-Jacques Roquebert, created a double-hulled vessel with a long, somewhat streamlined tower placed centrally on a flat deck. The outer hull was of distinctive canoe-style shape at each end, with a curved bow and saucer-shaped stern. The large rudder was set below the stern and another saucer-like extension from the keel. Its length of 92.3m (302.8ft) exceeded the operational depth of 80m (262ft). The pressure hull was of

riveted construction, using steel 16mm (0.62in) thick. The machinery consisted of two Schneider eight-cylinder double-acting diesel engines with a combined 4474kW (6000hp), and two Al23 electric motors. Fuel capacity was 320 tonnes (314.8t).

The boats were equipped with both 550mm (21.45in) and 400mm (15.7in) torpedo tubes, to be used according to the nature of the target ship. Four 550m tubes were placed forward, inside the hulls, a further three were mounted at deck level, aft of the tower, with two more at the stern, along with two 400mm tubes. The deck-mounted

Henri Poincaré
Dimensions: Length 92.3m (302.8ft), Beam 8.1m (26.7ft), Draught 4.4m (14.4ft)
Displacement (surface/submerged): 1572 tonnes (1547t) / 2092 tonnes (2059t)
Propulsion: two diesels of 2237kW (3000hp), two 839kW (1125hp) electric motors, two screws
Speed (surface/submerged): 17.5kt (32.4kmh, 20.1mph) / 10kt (19kmh, 12mph)
Range (surface/submerged): 14,000nm (25,928km, 16,111mi) at 7kt / 90nm (170km, 100mi) at 7kt
Armament (original): nine 550mm (21.45in), two 400mm (15.7in) torpedo tubes; one 100mm (3.9in) deck gun, two 13.2mm (0.5in) machine guns
Crew: 84

Henri Poincaré
The double-hulled *Redoutable* class was designed as an advance on the Requin boats and were heavily armed with torpedoes. Their function was that of surface raiders and defenders of the maritime supply line between France and its colonies. In World War II they did very little of either before most were scuttled.

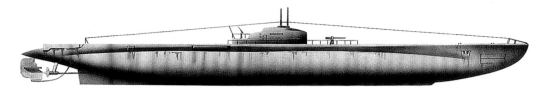

Casabianca
First based at Brest with the 2nd Division, Casabianca made two wartime patrols off Norway in 1940, then was deployed to Dakar in Senegal until October 1941. After escaping Toulon, it reached Algiers on 30 November 1942, and operated with the 8th Royal Navy Flotilla from Oran, sinking an Axis ASW patrol vessel.

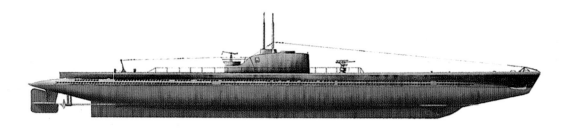

tubes could be swivelled within a
limited range but could not be reloaded
while the boat was submerged. Only
two reload torpedoes were carried. An
SM1925CA 100mm (3.9in) deck gun
was set forward of the tower, with a
twin SM14 13.2mm (0.5in) machine
gun mounted at the rear of the tower.
The midships and stern tubes were
located in a casing built upon the outer
hull. It took these large boats up to 60
seconds to dive.

In the first instance, only two of
the class were built, designated type
M-5.The next 29, designated M-6,
commissioned in regular batches
between 1930 and 1937, shared the
same vital statistics, but with slightly
increased power, with the last in the
class, *Casabianca*, powered by Sulzer
diesels of 3206.5kW (4300hp), and
Alsthom motors of 1566kW (2100hp).
The boats were built in numerous

shipyards, with consequent minor
differences.

From December 1942 the four
Redoutable-class submarines in Free
French control crossed to the United
States for refitting and modernization.
The smaller diameter tubes were
removed and replaced by a single
533mm (21in). The motors were
overhauled, new batteries installed,
and the pressure hulls and diving
auxiliaries reinforced. The ballast
tanks were altered to increase the
range. Efforts were made to improve
the soundproofing, as the class was
notably noisy. Radar and underwater
sound systems were installed, with
up-to-date sonar capabilities. Living
conditions were improved with
the installation of air conditioning
and a refrigerator. The tower was
modified, with the removal of the
elderly machine guns, which were

Rubis

The earlier boats had two tall telescopic radio masts. Some later ones had a 37mm (1.4in) gun abaft the tower as well as the main deck gun.

replaced with Oerlikon 20mm (0.79in)
AA guns. The telescopic masts were
also removed. The modernization work
was hampered by the lack of plans
and drawings. Also, the four surviving
submarines used two different types of
motor, Schneider/Sulzer.

Though mechanically reliable,
and good sea-boats, they were felt
to have poor resistance to depth
charging, especially in the case of the
hydroplanes; and to be insufficiently
equipped for the long cruises for
which they were designed, with poor
habitability other than for officers, and
a lack of food storage. Deployed to the
South Atlantic and the Far East, their
lack of air conditioning was a problem.

Sfax, a *Redoutable* class submarine, leaves Saint Nazaire, 1935. *Sfax* was one of three members of the class to be fitted with radio direction-finding.

'600' and '630' classes (1927–45)

French naval policy required an effective fleet of coastal submarines, particularly in the Mediterranean Sea, where Italy was considered a potential enemy.

This resulted in two main classes of broadly similar type, defined by their displacement tonnage. The basic specification was given by the Navy but design features varied according to the builder. The '600' class, built between 1923 and 1927, numbered 12, completed by 1930. Four were built in each of three yards, AC de la Loire, Nantes, under the direction of Jean-Ernest Simonot; Chantiers Augustin Normand, Le Havre, by Normand and Fernand Fenaux; and at Chantiers Schneider, Bordeaux by Maxime Laubeuf. The '630 tonne' class was formed of four distinct groups. Group I was five boats of the Schneider-Laubeuf type, including *Argonaute*; Group II, Normand-Fenaux type, nine boats; and Group III, Loire-Simonot type, two boats.

Double hull

All were double-hulled, with a sharply raked stem, some with a pronounced downwards-sloping foredeck. The tower was oblong, with varying profiles, but all had the bridge forward and a space behind for machine guns. A serrated cable cutter and net-evasion cable were fitted. Although the dimensions of the 630 class were slightly less than the 600s, the displacement was slightly greater, and habitability for the crew of 41 was improved. Operating depth was 80m (262ft).

Engines varied according to builder: Normand-Vickers, Schneider-Carel, Sulzer, but all were rated in the range 932kW (1250hp) (600-class) to 1044kW (1400hp) (630-class) giving a surface speed of 14kt. Electric motors of 746kW (1000hp) gave a submerged speed of 9kt. Fuel capacity, mostly held outside the pressure hull, was 61 tonnes (60t) in the 600s, and 96.5 tonnes (95t) in the 630s.

Weaponry

Torpedo armament in the '600' class consisted of seven 550mm (21.45) tubes, three forward (two external), two aft (both external), and two midships in a twin traversing mount. The '630s' had six 550mm (21.45in) tubes: three forward (two external), two midships in external traversing mounts; one aft in traversing mount. They also had two 400mm (15.7in) tubes located in traversing mounts aft. The torpedo load was nine. The arrangement of tubes suggested much surface action was envisaged, including commerce attacks with the 400mm torpedoes. All carried a light single gun on the foredeck: in the case of *Argonaute* a 75mm (3in) 35-cal

Schneider M1928, though boats of the 600' class had older models.

By 1939 the 600/630 class, especially the 600s, were obsolescent but all did wartime service with the exception of *Ondine* and *Nymphe*.

Argonaute (Group I)

Dimensions: Length 63.4m (208ft), Beam 6.4m (21ft), Draught 4.24m (13.9ft)

Displacement (surface/submerged): 630 tonnes (620t) / 798 tonnes (785t)

Propulsion: two Schneider-Carel diesels of 485kW (650hp), two 373kW (500hp) motors, two screws

Speed (surface/submerged): 14kt (26kmh, 16mph) / 9kt (17kmh, 10mph)

Range (surface/submerged): 4000nm (7408km, 4603mi) / 82nm (152km, 84.4mi)

Armament: six 550mm (21.45in) tubes, 13 torpedoes; two 400mm (15.7in) tubes, nine torpedoes; one 76mm (3in) 35cal deck gun; one 8mm (0.3in) machine gun

Crew: 41

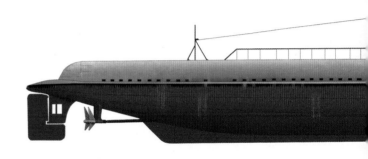

Ariane, seen here at Cherbourg, was lead boat of a sub-class of four '600' type built at the Augustin-Normand yard. It was scuttled at Oran on 9 November 1942.

Argonaute

Argonaute was a Schneider-Laubeuf design. Assigned to the Mediterranean squadron, it was sunk by British ships at Oran in November 1942.

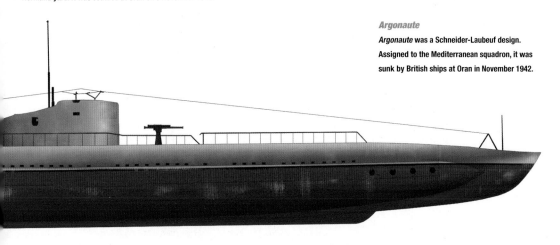

Requin

Class leader of a group of nine, built between 1923–1928. These were ocean-going boats of 1168 tonnes (1150t) surfaced. They had ten 550mm (21.65in) tubes, of which four were deck-mounted. All underwent refits in 1936, including new 100mm Model 1928 deck guns designed for submarines.

TORPEDO RANGE

The 1500 class fired torpedoes of 550mm (21.45in) diameter, driven by compressed air, which left a trail of surface bubbles. They carried a 310kg (683lb) charge of TNT and had a range of 3000m (3300yd) at 45kt, or 7000m (7650yd) at 35kt. By 1939 some versions had a range extended to 4000m (4400yd) or 8000m (8750yd). The 400mm (15.7in) type carried a 144kg (317lb) warhead, with range of 2000m (2200yd) at 44kt and 3000m (3800yd) at 35kt. They had alcohol-fuelled wet-heater turbine engines.

Espadon

A *Requin*-class boat, commissioned in 1927. Drawing on WWI experience, both French and German, these double-hulled boats were precursors of the '600' and '630' types, which were designed under greater restraints.

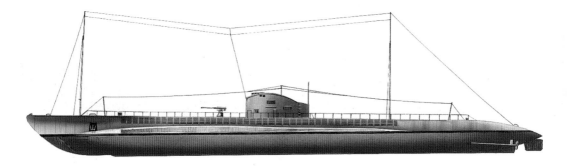

Galathée

This was a coastal boat of the *Sirène*-class, displacing 619 tonnes (609t) on the surface, with seven 550mm tubes (two external). Commissioned in 1927, it was scuttled in 1942 and refloated to be used first by the Italians, then the Germans.

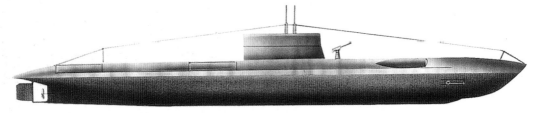

Surcouf (1929)

The large 'cruiser-submarine' was an idea that took hold in several navies. However, the great French experiment was not a military success.

Until Japan built even bigger ones, *Surcouf* was the largest submarine in the world. Its design began as 'Project Q' in 1926, under Jean-Jacques Roquebert, who also designed the *Redoutable* class. Launched at the Cherbourg arsenal in 1929 and commissioned in December 1932, after long trials, it was intended to be the prototype of a squadron of up to 16 similar vessels.

Its double hull, an enlarged *Redoutable*, was a bold attempt at combining the stealth qualities of a submarine with the surface fighting and scouting ability of a cruiser. It was also a means of evading the obligations of the Washington Naval Treaty of 1921, which placed no limitations on submarine size or construction. From within the pressure hull, it could fire from four 550mm (21.45in) torpedo tubes. Two partially trainable triple casings at deck level held one 550mm and two 400mm (15.7in) tubes. All were ready-loaded and 12 torpedoes were held in reserve. In a watertight shielded casing merged with the tower two Model 1924 203mm (8in) guns were housed, able to sink a destroyer

Surcouf, carrying the designation number 17P, close to the Royal Navy's submarine base at Faslane, on the Firth of Clyde, in 1940.

Surcouf

Dimensions: Length 110m (361ft), Beam 9m (29.5ft), Draught 7.25m (23.75ft)

Displacement (surface/submerged): 3300 tonnes (3250t) / 4373 tonnes (4304t)

Propulsion: two diesels of 2834kW (3800hp), two 1250kW (1700hp) electric motors, two screws

Speed (surface/submerged): 18.5kt (34.3kmh, 21.3mph) / 10kt (19kmh, 12mph)

Range (surface/submerged): 10,000nm (18,520km, 11,508mi) at 10kt / 59nm (130km, 81mi) at 4.5kt

Armament: eight 550mm (21.45in) tubes, 14 torpedoes; four 400mm (15.7in) tubes, eight torpedoes; twin 203mm (8in) guns, two 37mm (1.4in) AA guns, four 13.2mm (0.5in) machine guns

Crew: 118

or even a light cruiser. Secondary armament consisted of four Hotchkiss 8mm (0.3in) guns. A watertight hangar in the rear of the large superstructure held a Besson MB-41-0 floatplane (Type M-41-1 from 1933) with a range of 400km (234mi), able in pre-radar days to relay the location of an enemy and monitor its movements. It was deposited in and lifted from the water by a folding derrick. *Surcouf* also carried a 5m (16.4ft) motorboat and had accommodation for 40 additional persons, troops or prisoners.

It was powered by two Sulzer diesels of a combined 5667kW (7600hp), and two Alsthom electric motors of a combined 2535kW (3400hp). The service speed was 18.5kt, though it was capable of 20kt, enabling it to act as a fleet escort if required. Operating depth was 80m (262ft) so that a boat 110m (360ft) long had to dive somewhat carefully. *Surcouf* could go down to 180m (590ft) and crush depth was reckoned as 480m (1574ft).

Surcouf's main guns could fire an HE shell of 116kg (254lb) a distance of 13.72km (15,000yd) at an elevation of 10°. But their use and effectiveness were very much determined by sea conditions and the extent to which the turret could be trained to bear.

Armament
The 203mm (8in) guns and gun-laying equipment were not new, as many guns in good condition were available from decommissioned surface ships. The twin turret weighed 185 tonnes (182 tons) and could be ready to fire within three minutes of surfacing, sending a 120kg (264lb) shell a distance of 27,500m (90,223ft).

Surcouf

Described as a 'corsair-submarine', *Surcouf* was intended as a commerce raider, equipped with a Besson MB411 floatplane and a 4.5m (15ft) motorboat, and with room to hold around 40 prisoners. Its cruising endurance was a maximum 90 days. Its designers did not anticipate attacks from the air, as it took two minutes to dive.

Floatplane
A Besson MB-41-0 floatplane with a 400km (248 mile) range was originally carried in a hangar behind the tower. After a crash-landing in July 1933 it was replaced by an MB-41-1 model. Both were wood-framed. In 1938 a Breguet gyroplane was tested as a possible replacement.

Colour scheme
Originally painted in French naval grey, *Surcouf* was repainted in 'dark Prussian blue' from 1934 until 1940. From then it was painted in two-tone grey.

This photograph shows the gun turret without the streamlined casing that was fitted for seagoing service.

Holding cell
The space allocated to holding 40 prisoners, or troops, could also be used for storing materials.

Oberon and Odin class (1927–45)

HMS *Oberon* marked the beginning of a new generation of post-World War I British submarines.

Built for long-range patrol duties, and commissioned in 1927, *Oberon* was the first RN submarine to be named rather than just numbered. Its design drew on the L-class of World War I, but a range of improvements made it a very different craft. Although it has been regarded as the lead ship of the O-class, there were significant differences between it and its successors. Design work was done by the Vickers company.

O-class

The O-class was single-hulled with saddle tanks that held both fuel and seawater ballast. The pressure hull was formed of 19mm (0.75in) steel, a thickness which allowed a depth of 150m (500ft), but this may have been for general robustness against depth charges as it was not known to have gone below 61m (200ft): already an exceptional depth for the time. The tower was a substantial construction, mounting a 102mm (4in) gun on an open platform forward of and just below the bridge, and with a high telescopic radio mast, the aerial linked to a low T-pole at the stern.

The engines were Admiralty-type six-cylinder diesels, with a combined 2013kW (2700bhp), and two electric motors rated at 1010kW (1350shp). Three battery compartments held 336 cells. Operational speed was 13.75kt surfaced, slower than the design speed of 15kt, and 7.5kt submerged. *Oberon* carried 189 tonnes (186t) of fuel oil. The saddle tanks, originally riveted to the hull, prone to leakage and vulnerable to depth charges, were replaced by welded tanks in 1937.

Crew accommodation was in the spartan British tradition. Though the class was originally intended for Far East service, which did not happen in *Oberon's* case, there was scant, if any, special preparation for tropical conditions.

Eight 533mm (21in) torpedo tubes were fitted, six in the bow and two in the stern, and 16 torpedoes were carried. The deck gun was a 102mm (4in) QF MkIV, and two single Vickers 12.7mm (0.5in) liquid-cooled machine guns were mounted on pintles at either side of the tower.

The improvements in instrumentation made during the 1920s were one reason for *Oberon's* large size. It was the first submarine with ASDIC installed from the start.

HMS *Odin*

Dimensions: Length 86.4m (283.7ft), Beam 9.1m (30ft), Draught 4.8m (15.7ft)

Displacement (surface/submerged): 1810 tonnes (1781t) / 2060 tonnes (2030t)

Propulsion: two Admiralty diesels of 1640kW (2200hp); two 492kW (660hp) electric motors, two screws

Speed (surface/submerged): 17.5kt (32.4kmh, 20.1mph) / 9kt (17kmh, 10mph)

Range (surface/submerged): 8400nm (15,557km, 9667mi) at 10kt / 70nm (130km, 81mi) at 4kt

Armament: eight 533mm (21in) torpedo tubes, 14 torpedoes; one QF 102mm (4in) deck gun; two 7.7mm (0.303in) Lewis guns

Crew: 56

HMS *Odin*

The O-class is more properly named after HMS *Odin* than *Oberon*, which was shorter, lighter and less powerful than the subsequent boats. Apart from *Odin*, *Orpheus* and *Oswald* were also sunk by Italian destroyers, and *Olympus* struck a mine off Malta.

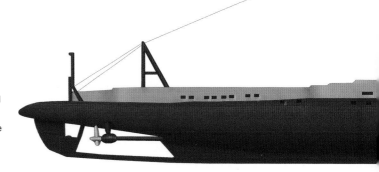

HMS *Oberon*

Dimensions: Length 82m (270ft), Beam 8.5m (28ft), Draught 4.6m (13.2ft)

Displacement (surface/submerged): 1332 tonnes (1311t) / 1922 tonnes (1892t)

Propulsion: two Vickers diesels of 1099kW (1475hp), two 260kW (350hp) electric motors, two screws

Speed (surface/submerged): 15kt (27.8kmh, 17.3mph) / 9kt (17kmh, 10mph)

Range (surface/submerged): 5000nm (9260km, 5755mi) at 9.5kt / 60nm (111km, 69mi) at 4kt

Armament: eight 533mm (21in) torpedo tubes, 16 torpedoes; one QF 102mm (4in) deck gun; two 7.7mm (0.303in) Lewis guns

Crew: 56

DIVING DEPTH

The deep diving capacity of some British submarine classes of the 1930s was a consequence of strengthening the pressure hulls against depth charges, rather than any wish to have the boats operate regularly at depths far below attack levels. On *Odin*-class test dives to 90m (300ft), deflections of the hull were noted and additional stiffening was provided. Any additional weight of course affected submerged speed, so greater depth for its own sake was not desirable.

HMS *Oberon*

Completed in 1927, *Oberon* was of an advanced design for the period, and with up-to-date instrumentation. One defect was the riveted saddle tanks, which contained additional fuel, but tended to leave a trail of leakage. Placed in reserve between 1937 and 1939, it was used in World War II primarily for training, and decommissioned in July 1944.

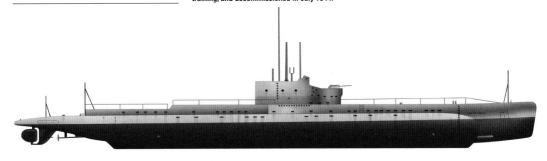

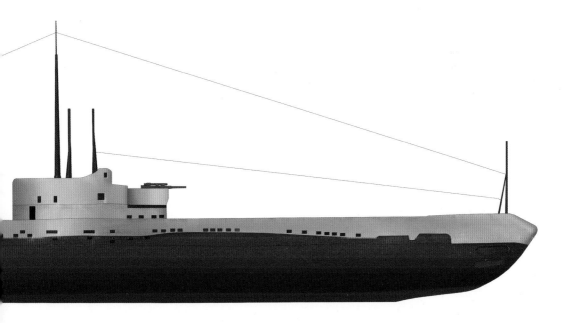

It had Type 709 hydrophones, a Type SF direction finder and the most up-to-date form of periscope. In its wartime service as a training craft, the boat was fitted with an Oerlikon 20mm (0.79in) AA cannon and a Type 291W radio direction finder. *Oberon* was built in the Admiralty yard at Chatham. Two others, *Otway* and *Oxley*, were built simultaneously at the Vickers yard in Barrow, differing in that they were 1.3m (4.5ft) longer, had Vickers diesel engines delivering 2237kW (3000bhp), and fuel storage for 240 tonnes (236t).

Bigger boats

Some historians consider the six other O-boats as really a separate class. All were commissioned in 1929, all with Vickers engines. They were larger, longer and wider (see *Odin's* specifications). The extra space was primarily to accommodate more powerful engines: eight-cylinder four-cycle blast-injection type, developing

3281kW (4400bhp). These met the required service speed of 17.5kt surfaced. Much had been learned about the effects of different sea-water densities on the behaviour of a submarine, and the Odin boats' ballast and buoyancy system was designed to enable diving in fresh or lightly saline water as well as the deep sea (specific gravity of 1.00 to 1.30). They test-dived to 100m (330ft).

Parthian class

Very similar to the Odin class and also designed for long-range patrol in the Far East, the six Parthian-class boats (1929 had a more bulbous bow, were slightly longer and with diesels uprated to 3430kW (4600hp). Tankage of 161 tonnes (159t) enabled a range of 8400nm (15,557km, 9667mi) at 10kt. The deck gun was shielded and in the case of *Perseus* was a more up-to-date Mk X.

Opposite: HMS *Oberon* and three other O-class submarines alongside the depot ship HMS *Maidstone* in the early 1940s. The location is probably Algiers, where Maidstone was based in 1942–43.

HMS *Parthian*

Dimensions: Length 88.14m (289.2ft), Beam 9.12m (29.11ft), Draught 4.85m (16ft)
Displacement (surface/submerged):
1788 tonnes (1760 tons); 2072 tonnes (2040 tons))
Propulsion: two Admiralty diesels of 1640kW (2200hp); two 492kW (660hp) electric motors, two screws
Speed (surface/submerged): 17.5kt (32.4kmh, 20.1mph) / 9kt (17kmh, 10mph)
Range (surface/submerged): 8400nm (15,557km, 9667mi) at 10kt / 70nm (130km, 81mi) at 4kt
Armament: eight 533mm (21in) torpedo tubes, 14 torpedoes; one QF 102mm (4in) deck gun
Crew: 53

HMS *Parthian*

New higher-capacity batteries gave the *Parthian* class greater underwater endurance. If not carrying mines, they took 14 torpedoes of the standard British Mark VIII type. *Parthian* sank the Italian submarine *Diamante* on 20 June 1940 and the Vichy French *Souffleur* on 25 June 1941, as well as numerous Axis merchant vessels.

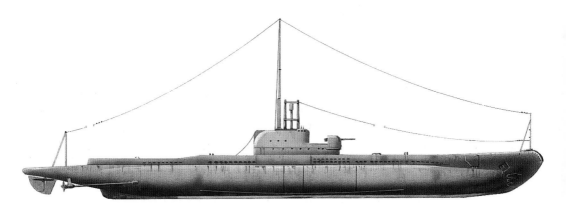

THE WARTIME ASDICS TYPE 129 AND TYPE 138

The Asdic (sonar in US parlance) that was to become familiar to all Royal Navy World War II submariners was the Type 129. First trialled inside a dome set in the front end of the keel of HMS *Seawolf* in 1937, in 1938 it was adopted as the standard submarine set. It was duly installed in all the submarines of the T-, U- and V-classes.

Operating at the now standard 10kHz, it was fitted in a cylindrical cage with a streamlined dome underneath the forward torpedo tubes at the fore-edge of the keel, with power from an electric motor inside a watertight tank that was itself inside the pressure hull. This enabled the oscillator unit to be pulled inside the submarine for maintenance, repair or exchange. The Type 129 was gyro-stabilized and intended as an attack set. Another of its potential uses was its SST (submerged sound telegraphy) capabilities. With this, a submarine could both pick up a very low-frequency message and get a bearing on the transmitting boat. In early versions, transmission was by Morse key and ranging was done by chronoscope, but the sets were soon modified to have a range recorder, A/S3, with automatic transmission.

An ASDIC-fitted submarine needed to reduce its own sound level, most of which came from its propellers, and trials had been conducted shortly before the war to try and reduce this source. Experiments were made with two S class submarines fitted with a form of ducted propeller, but not pursued. The best solution was adopted in the T-class submarines where the machinery was mounted on resilient fixings.

Mounted forward, the Type 129 had a blind stern arc, and from 1943, a passive, manually trained Type 138 hydrophone was added to cover the blind area. In T-class boats the Type 138 was fitted on the after casing between Nos. 9 and 10 tubes, with the set shoe-horned into the already packed engine room.

HMS *Porpoise* and Grampus class (1930–46)

This class was specifically designed as a minelayer. One of the values of minelaying from submarines is that it could be done secretly, so long as the submarine was not observed.

The immediate precursor was HMS *Porpoise* (1932), but the five *Grampus* class boats had significant differences. *Porpoise* had welded saddle tanks and its hull form was based on the P-class. The Grampus boats' double-hulled design was based on the T-class, though with some streamlining. *Porpoise* carried its fuel in the saddle tanks but in the *Grampus* boats, the bunkers were inside the pressure hull, with a capacity ranging from 120–149 tonnes (119–147t).

All six were driven by Admiralty-type vertical four-stroke blast-injection six-cylinder diesel engines of a combined 2461kW (3300bhp), and two electric motors in tandem on each shaft, developing 1215kW (1630bhp). Three battery sets of 112 cells, weighing 141 tonnes (139t). gave a submerged endurance of 66nm (122km, 76mi) at 4kt.

Fifty Mk XVI mines were carried in a non-watertight casing above the pressure hull, set on an endless chain-and-rack system which moved them at a controlled speed to discharge vents set in the stern. There were no stern torpedo tubes, but six forward, with 12 torpedoes. *Porpoise* had a 119mm (4.7in) deck gun, changed to 102mm (4in) as on the *Grampus* class. *Rorqual*, the only one to survive the war, was modified between 1941 and 1943 to carry 12 Mk2 mines, fired from the tubes.

Later orders for boats of this class were cancelled when mines dischargeable through torpedo tubes became readily available. The minelayers were then used as supply boats, especially in the Mediterranean, where they ran missions to Malta with the former mine deck packed with supplies.

HMS *Porpoise*

Dimensions: Length 88m (289ft), Beam 9.09m (29.8ft), Draught 4.83m (15.8ft)

Displacement (surface/submerged): 1796 tonnes (1768t) / 2067 tonnes (2035t)

Propulsion: two diesels of 1250kW (1650hp), two 610kW (815hp) electric motors, two screws

Speed (surface/submerged): 15.5kt (28.7kmh, 17.8mph) / 8.75kt (16.2kmh, 10mph)

Range (surface/submerged): 6300nm (11,667km, 7251mi) at 10.6kt / 64nm (118km, 73.6mi) at 4kt

Armament: six 533mm (21in) torpedo tubes, 12 torpedoes; 50 mines; one 202mm (4in) deck gun, two 7.7mm (0.303in) Lewis guns

Crew: 59

HMS *Porpoise*

Porpoise was recognizable from the others in its class by the external fuel tanks terminating about 18m (60ft) short of the bow structure. They served at various times in the West Indies, the Mediterranean and the China Station. Five were lost in World War II, including *Porpoise* itself, sunk by Japanese aircraft in the Malacca Straits on 19 January 1945.

MINES

The RN minelayers carried specially designed Mk XVI mines, of Herz horn contact type, with a charge of 145kg (320lb) of TNT. They were of hydrostatic type, designed for the mine and its sinker to go to the seabed, where the mine would be released and rise on its cable. When the hydrostat reached the preset level (anywhere between 1.4m (5ft) and 60m (90ft), it dropped off and the mine remained moored in position.

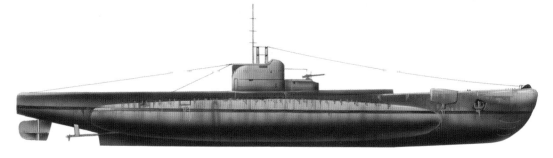

River class (1931–35)

This small class of three was the Royal Navy's final attempt at a fleet submarine. In the context of the RN's need to be a global force, a submarine of sufficient size, speed and endurance to accompany a battle fleet seemed to be desirable.

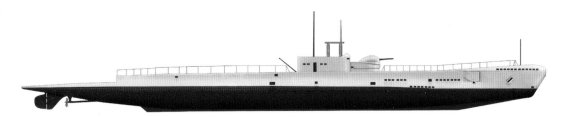

A new class, putting into effect all that had been learned in the previous decade, 20-strong, was planned. It was a double-hull design except that the riveted pressure hull came right to the keel, giving an unusual 'keyhole' shape in cross-section.

Streamlining

This was the era when streamlining became an essential aspect of fast-moving machines, and the Rivers presented an elegantly rounded form of superstructure, with minimal encumbrances on the long deck and the gun, set on a forward extension of the tower, shielded in a trainable turret.

As ever in submarine design, compromises had to be made in order to secure the prime design requirement, which in this case was speed. Stern torpedo tubes were dropped in order to save weight, and the pressure hull plating was 1.75kg/cm² (25psi), allowing for an operational depth of 60m (200ft) and a maximum depth of 91m (300ft).

To achieve a surface speed of 22.5kt (a record at the time), two vertical four-stroke blast injection

10-cylinder diesels of Admiralty design, developing a total power of 5965kW (8000bhp) at 400rpm, were installed. Using two auxiliary generators, driven by two Paxman-Ricardo sleeve-valve engines, the main engines could be supercharged to give a total of 7457kW (10,000bhp).

HMS Thames

Two 12m (40ft) periscopes were mounted in a frame, with a high telescopic radio mast just aft. The boats carried Type 118 ASDIC.

HMS *Thames*
Dimensions: Length 105m (345ft), Beam 8.61m (28.3ft), Draught 4.85m (15.9ft)
Displacement (surface/submerged): 2199.6 tonnes (2165t) / 2723 tonnes (2680t)
Propulsion: two supercharged diesels of 3750kW (5000hp), two 950kW (1250hp) electric motors, two screws
Speed (surface/submerged): 22k (41kmh, 25mph) / 10kt (19kmh, 11.5mph)
Range (surface/submerged): 12,000nm (22,224km, 13,809mi) at 12kt / 118nm (218.5mi, 136mi) at 4kt
Armament: six 533mm (21in) torpedo tubes, 12 torpedoes; one 102mm (4in) QF gun
Crew: 61

DRIVE SYSTEMS
Apart from the U/V class, RN submarines deployed in World War II had direct drive: each diesel engine was linked by a drive shaft via a clutch to a double armature electric motor. A shaft from this, via another clutch ('tail clutch') turned the propeller shaft. By disengaging the diesel engine from the drive shaft, the boat could run on the electric motors only, drawing power from the batteries. With the tail clutch disengaged, the diesels could be used to charge the batteries. With diesel-electric drive, the diesel engines are not connected to the propeller shaft. They act as electricity generators, to power electric motors that turn the propeller shafts.

Their performance was not wholly satisfactory, leading to a power de-rating of about 20 per cent. Fuel oil capacity was 219 tonnes (216t) of fuel oil in external welded tanks. The electric motor room was between the main and auxiliary engine rooms, and the main motors, one on each shaft, developed a total of 1864kW (250bhp) at 245rpm at a 75-minute rating and 984kW (1320bhp) at 2-hour rating.

Slow speeds were obtained with the main motor armatures in series developing up to 37kW (50bhp) per shaft at 35rpm, giving a submerged speed of 10kt. Three battery tanks had 112 cells each, 336 cells in total. They were large capacity Chloride E1 68601 type with a discharge rate of

3910 ampere hours for 1 hour, 6860 ampere hours for 5 hours and 7830 ampere hours for 10 hours. The total weight was approximately 222 tons.

Crew space was more generous than usual due to the lack of stern tubes, which allowed for an aft crew compartment above the compressed air cylinders.

The torpedo armament consisted of six 533mm (21-inch) bow tubes. A 119mm (4.7-in) gun was originally fitted, but in keeping with submarine policy of the period was changed, after completion, to a 102mm (4-in) QF gun with 120 rounds of ammunition.

The main differences in *Severn* from *Thames* were an increase in

length of the motor room consequent on a change from the 330-volt battery grouping in *Thames* to a 220-volt grouping. The two escape chambers and main bulkheads were constructed to withstand a test pressure of 4.9kg/cm^2 (70psi) instead of 2.45kg/cm^2 (35psi). The internal oil fuel tank was deleted, and the hull structure was strengthened around the main engine room.

S-class (1931–45)

The Royal Navy's largest class of submarine, 62 S-class submarines were built in total.

In design, appearance and production they again form three groups, with two sets commissioned in the 1930s, and the largest group of 50 between 1940 and 1945. The basic design was an Admiralty one, single-hulled, based in part on the WWI L-class. Group I displaced 738.6 tonnes (727t) / 952 tonnes (937t). They were intended for service in northern seas, with an

initial range of 3800nm (7038km, 4374mi) and an endurance period of up to 10 days. Any increase would have required larger fuel tanks and space for more powerful radio equipment. The original design was constrained by the terms of the 1930 naval agreement, and the designers struggled to keep the displacement weight low. As it was, the first two

HMS *Storm*

Storm was commissioned in July 1943. These were the first British submarines fitted with radar for surface as well as for air search. *Storm* served in eastern waters, with a ballast tank converted to fuel-holding to allow for the lengthy patrols required.

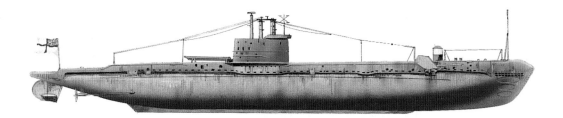

boats, with 39.5 tonnes (39t) of fuel held inside the pressure hull, were barely up to the demands of the wide Norway-Shetland exit route from the North Sea to the Atlantic.

The tower, elliptical in shape, was small and quite low. On the first eight, the bridge was enclosed, but in war service, this was changed to an open bridge. The deck gun was mounted on a low breastwork extending forward from the tower. There was no bow net-cutter, but a heavy wire cable stretched from the stem over the periscope columns to the stern. A telescopic radio mast was placed aft of the periscopes. The forward diving planes were folded to rise like a pair of ears above deck level. The flooding perforations around the bow show how the ends of the boat are built out fore and aft of the pressure hull. Until 1941 the S-boats had riveted hulls built on welded T-bar frames; from 1941, welded pressure hulls made from strengthened 'S' quality steel enabled diving to 107m (350ft).

The diesel engines were built to Admiralty design by the respective building yards. Two Admiralty eight-cylinder vertical four-stroke blast-injection diesels each developing

HMS Sanguine

Sanguine was the last 'S' class to be built and its commissioning coincided with the end of the war in Europe. It never saw active service. In a post-war refit a folding snorkel mast was fitted and the stern torpedo tube and the AA platform were removed. In 1958 it was sold to Israel as the Rahav.

578kW (775bhp) provided power to the first four boats, with two electric motors giving a continuous 969kW (1300bhp), or a one-hour burst to 1074kW (1440bhp). Two battery compartments each held 112 high-capacity cells, arranged in two sets of 56. Fuel capacity was 73 tonnes (72t).

HMS Sanguine was the last S-class submarine to be commissioned, in May 1945. Note the sonar dome and the absence of a deck gun in this photograph.

Six 533mm (21in) torpedo tubes were fitted, all in the bow, with a total of 12 torpedoes. A 76mm (3in) gun was briefly mounted in a casing on the superstructure of *Swordfish* but replaced in the interest of weight and balance by a 76mm (3in) deck gun, supplemented by a single 0.78mm (0.303in) machine gun.

Group II was formed of eight boats built between 1934 and 1937. They were 1.9m (6.2ft) longer and 30.5 tonnes (30t) heavier. For a time, their deck gun was in a mount which retracted into a forward extension of the tower. Dive depth at 90m (300ft) was as in Group I; range was upped to 6000nm (11,112km, 6906mi) at 10kt.

Group III, numbering 50 boats, launched in 1940–45. These were larger again (see Specifications). From 1940, 45 had an external stern 533mm (21in) tube fitted, and an Oerlikon 20mm

(0.79in) AA gun, mounted in a railed bandstand aft of the tower. In the final 18 boats, the stern tube was removed (perhaps to balance the insertion of a snorkel) and the 76mm (3in) deck gun was replaced by a 102mm (4in) gun. The 76mm guns were on the open deck but the larger gun was on a raised platform mount forward of the tower, with some shielding.

They also carried fuel in some of the ballast tanks, raising capacity to 99.5 tonnes (98t). Operational depth was down to 110m (350ft). From late 1941, the class was fitted with surface as well as air radar search.

Propulsion varied among the 50 boats in Group III. Most had eight-cylinder Admiralty or Scott diesels and GE or Metrovick electric motors. HMS *Storm* (1943) was driven by Brotherhood diesels and Metrovick electric motors.

HMS *Seraph* (Group III)

Dimensions: Length 66.1m (217ft), Beam 7.2m (23.75ft), Draught 4.5m (14.7ft)

Displacement (surface/submerged): 879 tonnes (865t) / 1010 tonnes (990t)

Propulsion: two diesels of 700kW (950bhp); two 435kW (650hp) electric motors, two screws

Speed (surface/submerged): 15kt (28kmh, 17mph) / 10kt (19kmh, 12mph)

Range (surface/submerged): 6000nm (11,112km, 6905mi) at 10kt / 120nm (220km, 140mi) at 3kt

Armament: seven 533mm (21in) torpedo tubes, 12 torpedoes; one 76mm (3in) deck gun, one 20mm (0.79in) AA gun

Crew: 48

Radio mast
A distinctive feature of RN submarines of this period was the tall telescopic radio and signalling mast.

HMS *Swordfish*
Commissioned in November 1932, *Swordfish* was among the first of the 'S' class, and as such was subject to various modifications through the 1930s, which were incorporated in later boats of the class.

Torpedo tubes
The first two 'S' class groups did not have a stern torpedo tube.

UNDERWATER TARGET

Rumours of Germany's Type XXI 'wonder weapon' led to hurried experimental work on HMS *Seraph* in mid-1944. *Seraph* was taken in for repairs and conversion to an underwater target. The modifications included the uprating of the main motors to 1193kW (1600shp) at full power, the fitting of coarser pitch propellers as on the T-class, allowing the extra power to be converted to thrust; and the installation of a high-capacity battery to extend endurance. To reduce drag, the hull was streamlined by fairing off all apertures and reducing the size of the hydroplanes. The forward planes were also fixed in the 'out' position and given a more powerful control mechanism. The forward periscope, radar mast, anti-aircraft guns, and deck gun were removed, and the profile of the conning tower was reduced. *Seraph's* drag was reduced by some 55 per cent, and mean submerged speed was up to 12.5kt at periscope depth, though this was still 3.5kt slower than the Type XXI. In terms of submerged endurance at lower speeds, *Seraph* could maintain 12kt for about 45 minutes, or 6kt for 8 hours, roughly double its pre-conversion endurance. Manoeuvrability was improved at higher speeds, even though the control surfaces had been reduced in area. While the modifications showed what was possible, the modified Seraph, unlike the Type XXI, was no longer of military value. Much more work was needed before a serious rival could be produced.

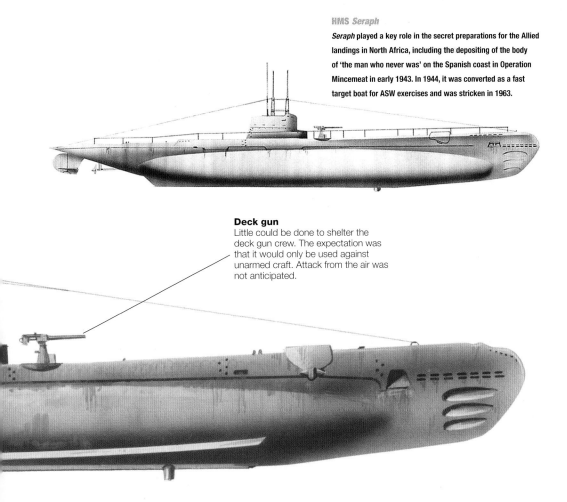

HMS *Seraph*

Seraph played a key role in the secret preparations for the Allied landings in North Africa, including the depositing of the body of 'the man who never was' on the Spanish coast in Operation Mincemeat in early 1943. In 1944, it was converted as a fast target boat for ASW exercises and was stricken in 1963.

Deck gun
Little could be done to shelter the deck gun crew. The expectation was that it would only be used against unarmed craft. Attack from the air was not anticipated.

T-class (1934–44)

This was another large class (53 boats) with boats launched in three phases. The original brief was for an ocean-going submarine of around 1200–1500t surfaced, with an endurance capability of 42 days and a large forward salvo of torpedoes.

While this remained unchanged, there were many variations between and within the groups. Group I consisted of 22 boats of riveted construction, single-hulled with saddle tanks. Diving depth was 91m (303ft). Two external bow tubes gave them a distinctive humped bow. The tower was of the same streamlined form as the S-class, with the deck gun mounted forward of and just below the bridge.

Originally the bridge was open, but was later enclosed in most Group I boats, only to be opened up again during war service, despite the spray that frequently drenched it. The pressure hull was divided by watertight bulkheads into six compartments. Escape hatches were located at either end.

Diesel power came from several manufacturers. Most had Vickers four-stroke engines. Boats built by Cammell Laird had Sulzer two-stroke engines, and the Royal Dockyards used Admiralty-type. Four from Scotts had MAN engines: these were replaced in wartime. All were of 930kW (1250bhp). Submerged propulsion was provided by 336-cell battery sets weighing 288 tonnes (283.4t), driving two 1080kW (1450bhp) Laurence Scott electric motors. These provided an endurance of 48 hours at 2.5kt (4.6kmh, 2.9mph) or one hour at the maximum submerged speed of 9kt (17kmh, 10mph). Fuel capacity was 133 tonnes (132t).

The T-class was formidably well-armed. Six internal forward tubes were supplemented by four forward-facing external tubes, two in the bow and two at the base of the tower. Sixteen torpedoes were carried. On eight of

The crew of the Royal Navy T-class submarine HMS *Thunderbolt* pose for a photograph beside the QF 102mm (4in) naval deck gun after returning to their base at Holy Loch in Scotland from patrol in the Bay of Biscay where it encountered and sank the Italian *Regia Marina Liuzzi* class submarine *Capitano Tarantini* on 15 December 1940, southwest of the Gironde Estuary near Bordeaux, France.

ESCAPE SYSTEMS

When a submarine was depth-charged, bombed or torpedoed, survivors were rare. It was an accepted hazard that most crews would perish with their boat. In the British Navy in World War II, some submarine classes had escape systems, others did not. Escape hatches were sometimes fitted (e.g. in HMS *Oberon* but not in the *Odin* boats) but commanders were known to bolt them from above to avoid blow-outs caused by depth charges. From the 1920s, Davis Submarine Escape Apparatus was available, consisting of a 'rubber lung', oxygen bottle with mouthpiece, and goggles; and from around 1930 escape chambers were included in at least some designs. The T-class had two, incorporated in the forward and aft bulkheads. Later came the 'twill trunk' – a tube of rubberized canvas, about 0.7m (2ft) in diameter, stowed below the escape hatch, which could be lowered into the compartment below, creating an air pocket in which the men could breathe even as the compartment was flooded in order to equalize the air and water pressure. One man had then to dip under the trunk and open a vent valve in the hatch, filling the trunk with water. One by one the men could put on their DSEA gear and go up the trunk, eventually reaching the surface. An RN medical report in 1945 concluded that "the method is useful only if the depth is not great and the air in the submarine is respirable after compression. Such conditions are unfortunately rare".

the Group I boats a single external stern-facing tube was added. The large increase in torpedo armament was due to the Admiralty's concern that more intensive ASW action deterred close-up attack and that a wider spread of torpedoes was needed to ensure getting a hit on a moving ship.

The original deck gun was a 102mm (4in) QF Mk XII or XXII and its breastwork was not armour-plated. In the after part of the tower three 7.8mm (0.303in) Lewis machine guns were originally carried, replaced in war service by Vickers VGO guns. Bren guns and 20mm (0.79in) Oerlikons were also used, depending on availability. In 1941 some Group I boats were fitted for minelaying via the torpedo tubes. Group II and III boats had welded hulls,

HMS *Thule*

HMS *Thule* was one of the 17 Group III T-class boats, commissioned in May 1944. It packed 10 torpedo tubes into a frame of the same displacement as the 'O' class.

formed in prefabricated sections which were combined on the launching berth. The forward external tubes were moved 2m (7ft) back, eliminating the bulbous bow. All were built with the external stern tube, and the two midship tubes were moved to fire aft, angled outwards about 70.

In order to serve in the Far East and Pacific, a number of Group II and III boats had their operating range increased to 9559nm (17,703km, 11,000mi) at 10kt. This was done by converting ballast tanks 3 and 5 to hold fuel, increasing capacity to 235.7 tonnes (230t). Two freon blower units were fitted for cooling, but condensation was a problem: one source reported that 181l (40gals) of water could be collected in 24 hours.

HMS *Truant* (1939) was the first RN submarine to be successfully fitted with a snorkel ('snort' in RN parlance). The T and S classes were both fitted with combined exhaust/induction snorkel masts.

From 1941, in addition to Type 129 ASDIC, fitted below the bow, the T-class were fitted with a deck-mounted DF detecting coil, Type 267 Seaguard and Type 291 Airguard radar. ASDIC Type 129 was fitted below and aft of the forward tubes, its dome protected by an obstruction rod.

HMS *Thule* (Group III)

Dimensions: Length 84.28m (276.5ft), Beam 7.77m (25.5ft), Draught 4.45m (14.6ft)

Displacement (surface/submerged): 1310 tonnes (1290t) / 1585 tonnes (1560t)

Propulsion: two diesels of 1900kW (2500hp), two 1080kW (1450hp) electric motors, two screws

Speed (surface/submerged): 15.5kt (28.7kmh, 17.8mph) / 9kt (17kmh, 10mph)

Range (surface/submerged): 4500nm (8334km, 5178mi) at 11kt / 121nm (224km, 139mi) at 2.5kt

Armament: 11 533mm (21in) torpedo tubes, six internal (forward) five external (aft-facing), 17 torpedoes; QF 102mm (4in) deck gun, one 20mm (0.79in), two 0.78mm (0.303in) AA guns

Crew: 61

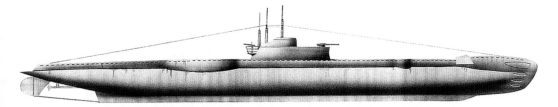

U-class (1936–45)

Planned in 1936, originally as unarmed training boats, the U-class was the Royal Navy's first diesel-electric submarine.

The first three, *Undine, Unity,* and *Ursula*, were modified during construction, with six internal and two external bow tubes. They were completed in 1938, with another 12 in 1940–41. A second group of 28 followed between 1940 and 1943, of very similar displacement but with 1.78m (5.75ft) longer sterns, and with four internal tubes only. These also had a more streamlined bow profile, as the bulge containing external tubes was eliminated. All but two (*Umpire* and *Una*) were built by Vickers at Barrow and Newcastle, and all were of riveted single-hull construction, of a maximum

0.78mm (0.5in) thickness, with all fuel and ballast tanks fitted inside, giving very cramped space. The hull was divided into six compartments, separated by watertight bulkheads. There were four hatches to the deck, with a 'twill trunk' hatch in the torpedo and engine rooms for escape. Operational depth was down to 61m (200ft), and the boats were highly manoeuvrable, particularly those of Group II. This agility helped them in attacks on enemy submarines.

These were the first RN submarines to have diesel-electric drive, dispensing with clutches and vibration dampers. Main power came from two Davey-Paxman RXS with welded steel frames. This engine type, in six-cylinder in-line format, was specially developed for use in submarines. Each produced 298kW (400bhp) at 825rpm, and each was coupled with a 275kW (368hp) generator via a Wellman-Bibby flexible coupling. Controls were mounted between the two engines.

The engines normally needed heavy maintenance when the boats returned from patrols. A 112-cell battery set was

U-Class Group I boats of original dimension:
Undine, Ursula, Unity, Umpire, Utmost

U-class Group I boats of length (196.25ft):
Umpire*, Una*, Unbeaten*, Undaunted*, Union *, Unique, Upholder, Upright, Urchin*, Urge*, Usk*

(* indicates no external tubes)

HMS *Undine* (Group 1)

Dimensions: Length 59.8m (190.6ft), Beam 4.8m (15.75ft), Draught 4.8m (15.75ft)

Displacement (surface/submerged): 640 tonnes (630t); 741.7 tonnes (730t)

Propulsion: Diesel electric: two diesels of 298kW (400hp), two 307kW (412hp) electric motors, two screws

Speed (surface/submerged): 11.25kt (20.8kmh, 12.9mph) / 9kt (16.7kmh, 10.3mph)

Range (surface/submerged): 4050nm (7500km, 4661mi) at 10kt / 23nm (42.6km, 26.5mi) at 8kt

Armament: four 533mm (21in) bow tubes, one 76mm (3in) deck gun; three 0.78mm (0.303in) machine guns

Crew: 27

---

*HMS **Undine***

Altogether, 49 U-class boats were commissioned into the RN. A further 21 served in other navies. Most U-class submarines were attached to the 10th flotilla at Malta, and 16 were lost in the Mediterranean.

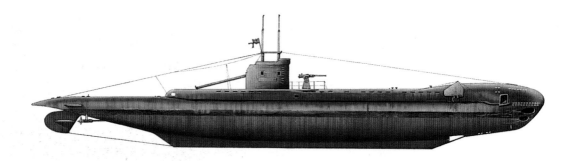

TORPEDOES

The primary torpedo used by Royal Navy submarines was the Mark VIII** variant (asterisks indicating 3rd modification), though shortages led to some submarines using the older Mark IV in the early stages. It weighed 1566kg (3452lb) with a 365kg (805lb) warhead, powered by a Brotherhood burner-cycle engine, the world's first, in which air at a pressure of around 59 kg/cm^2 (840 lb/in^2) was heated to 1000°C (1800°F) by burning a small amount of atomized shale oil fuel. This mixture was fed into the engine through poppet valves and its spontaneous ignition gave a greater propulsive efficiency than any contemporary torpedo of a similar size. Its range was 4570m (5000yd) at 45.5kt (84.3kmh, 52.4mph) or 6400m (7000yd) at 41kt (76kmh, 47mph). Its hit rate during the war, reckoned at 1040 definite hits for 5421 torpedoes fired, was remarkable. The Mark VIII was primarily fitted with a contact detonator which fired upon impact. A magnetic non-contact pistol of CCR (Compensated Coil Rod) type was also developed and used during the war. Mark VIII would remain the standard torpedo used by the T-class (and all Royal Navy submarines) until 1971.

carried. Fuel storage capacity was 38 tonnes (36.6t). The first seven of the class had two additional bow tubes, mounted externally. Total torpedo load was 10. A single deck gun was fitted close to the tower, as the design omitted an ammunition hatch: a QF 12-pdr (76mm) in the earliest boats, later a 76mm (3in) gun.

A jumping antenna was fitted in the tower for infrasound signals at periscope depth, and a telescopic 8m (27ft) WT mast. Search and attack periscopes, 200mm (8in) bifocal and 150mm (6in) low power respectively, extendable only to 3.7m (12ft). Type 129 ASDIC was fitted to the U-class, with one set of hydrophones fitted forward and another on the tower.

RN submariners loading a torpedo at the Malta naval base. The Mark VIII was by far the most frequently used torpedo type by the British in World War II.

BRITISH PERISCOPES

When the submarine fleet began to be modernized in the late 1920s, with a special focus on the long-range operations demanded by the Far East station, new periscopes were developed for the O-class submarines: the CK2 binocular search periscope with sky search capability and the CH21 bifocal attack periscope. CK8 and CK9 binocular search periscopes and CH51 and CH55 bifocal attack periscopes were fitted in the T- and U-classes in the late 1930s. It was the latter group that was the standard fit in British submarines throughout World War II, although improvements were made along the way. The most important was a method to reduce the loss of light in the periscope column. By 1940 makers Barr and Stroud had developed a surface coating to increase the light transmission by about 60 per cent, greatly improving both day and night-time vision. In 1941 the Admiralty ordered that all submarine periscopes be 'bloomed' with this coating. Another development was an air blast technique to clear the window of the search periscopes when they were blinded by sea spray.

V-class (1941–58)

A highly successful type, V-class attack submarines that survived the war served several navies into the 1950s.

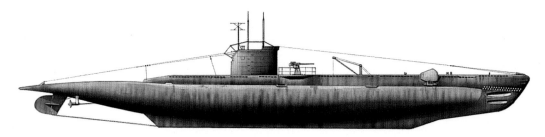

The V-class was a modification of the U-class, designed in 1941 to be built faster and with greater diving strength than their predecessors. The official designation was 'V-class long hull'. Eight were initially ordered and in all 22 were completed. All were built by Vickers. Resemblance to the U-class was close, but the V-class had a sharper bow design, were 2.4m (8ft) longer, and most importantly the pressure hulls were of 19mm (0.75in) steel rather than 12.7mm (0.5in), and welding was extensively used in construction, allowing an operating depth of 95m (312ft).

Powerplant

All had diesel-electric propulsion as with the U-class. Armament was four bow-mounted 533mm (21in) torpedo tubes, with 8–10 torpedoes, and a single 76mm (3in) deck gun.

HMS *Venturer*, with Lieutenant James Launders in command, used its Type 129 ASDIC for an hour, in hydrophone effect mode, while it stalked Type IXD2 U-864 off Norway on 9 February 1945, before becoming the first and only submarine so far to sink another submarine while both were below the surface.

HMS *Vagabond*

Dimensions: Length 62m (203.4ft), Beam 4.8m (15.75ft), Draught 4.8m (15.75ft)

Displacement (surface/submerged): 681 tonnes (670t) / 752 tonnes (740t)

Propulsion: Diesel electric: two diesels of 298kW (400hp), two 307kW (412hp) electric motors, two screws

Speed (surface/submerged): 11.25kt (20.84kmh, 12.95mph) / 10kt (19kmh, 12mph)

Range (surface/submerged): 4700nm (8704km, 5410mi) at 10kt / 30nm (55.5km, 34.5mi) at 9kt

Armament: four 533mm (21in) torpedo tubes, eight torpedoes; one 76mm (3in) 50cal deck gun; three 0.78mm (0.303in) machine guns

Crew: 33

HMS *Vagabond*

Commissioned on 19 September 1944, Vagabond was powered by two 6-cylinder Davey-Paxman engines generating 298kW (400hp) compared to the original U-class's 229kW (307hp) Admiralty diesels. Diving depth was 91m (300ft). V-boats carried the DF loop at the rear of the tower casing, not on top as in the U-class.

ASBESTOS

Asbestos, prized for its fire-resistant qualities, was widely used in submarine building and running, sometimes in unexpected ways. Palladized asbestos was incorporated in the catalytic scrubbers that reduced hydrogen in the X-crafts' battery exhaust. Asbestos was one of the substances used in anechoic coating of submarine hulls, and also in internal fireproofing.

UNITED KINGDOM

X-class midget submarines (1942–45)

The Italians, Japanese and British all made extensive use of very small two- to four-man submarines, for secret penetration of protected anchorages and bases.

The RN's versions were known as X-craft, developed under tight security from Varley Marine mini-subs built for river work. The first operational type was X-3 (1942). X-5 was built by Vickers at Barrow in the winter of 1942–43. It had all the key features of a full-size submarine incorporated in a hull 15.5m (51ft) long, with a loaded surface displacement of around 37 tonnes (35t). The hull, formed of welded 0.703kg (1.5lb) 'S' type steel, was formed of three sections, bolted together. It had a 'wet and dry' airlock hatch for a diver in addition

---

HMS X-5

Dimensions: Length 15.6m (51.25ft), Beam 1.75m (5.75ft), Draught 1.6m (5.3ft)

Displacement (surface/submerged): 27.4 tonnes (27t) / 30.48 tonnes (30t)

Propulsion: one diesel of 31.3kW (42hp); one 22.3kW (30hp) electric motor, single screw

Speed (loaded: surface/submerged): 6.5kt (12kmh, 7.5mph) / 5kt (9.2kmh, 5.1mph)

Range (loaded): 1320nm (2444km, 1519mi) at 4kt / 80nm (148km, 92mi) at 2kt

Armament: two 2000kg (4400lb) detachable charges

Crew: four

Sub-Lt K.C.J. Robinson uses the periscope of an X-craft while training in Rothesay Bay, Scotland.

HMS X-5

The side-mounted explosive charges had a central explosive chamber flanked by buoyancy chambers. They needed to have pressure-resistant casings with free-flooding ballast chambers so that they would sink as soon as released. The casing proved to be susceptible to leaks from seawater.

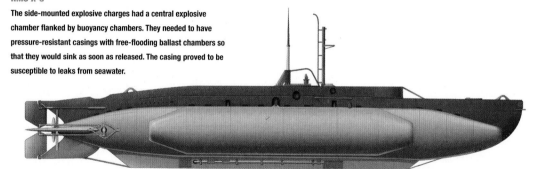

99

to a surface hatch. Though intended for use in relatively shallow water, it was tested down to 90m (295ft). It was also highly manoeuvrable, able to move submerged in all directions except sideways. It was powered by a four-cylinder Gardner 31kW (42hp) diesel engine and driven underwater by a Keith Blackman electric motor from a battery set of 112 Exide 20SP cells. Equipment included air compressor, gyro (Browns A) and magnetic (ACO MkXX) compasses (the latter external on a retractable pole), an AFV 6A/602 direction indicator, a Type 159 target indicator, a specially developed hydrophone, Browns auto-helmsman, a night and an attack periscope. Bolted on each side were its mine-type warloads: cased amatol explosive charges each of two tons, to be released from inside and deposited beneath a target vessel.

A single hydroplane was fitted at the stern, across the rudder which was divided in two to allow this. An air induction mast for the diesel engine was folded against the hull for submerged running. Habitability was at the bottom of the scale even given the expectation that missions would be relatively short. The X-craft would be towed, usually by a submarine, to its starting point (across the North Sea in X-5's case) while manned by a 'passage crew' who would then hand over to the mission crew. Hopefully with mission accomplished, it would rendezvous with the towboat for the voyage home.

The X-craft had only a single exit hatch, creating huge operational risks for the crew.

PAINTWORK AND CAMOUFLAGE

The standard scheme for RN submarines was grey sides and black upper surfaces and this continued through the war for Home Fleet boats. During WORLD WAR II, the camouflage scheme for submarines operating in the Mediterranean was light and dark green, but dark blue appears also to have been used, and some were even painted pink (a shade favoured by the future Admiral Lord Mountbatten). In the Far East, dark olive green was the standard colour.

Orzel (1936–40)

Orzel was one of Poland's two large patrol submarines. At the outbreak of war, Poland had a small submarine contingent, five minelayers and two quite up-to-date patrol craft.

In September 1939, as Germany invaded Poland, *Orzel* was dramatically navigated out of the Baltic and across the North Sea to Britain. Built at the De Schelde shipyard in Rotterdam, its design owed quite a lot to the Netherlands Navy's Class 0-16 submarine, which was completed in 1936. The Dutch Navy's chief engineer, G. de Rooij, was an advocate of hydraulics and numerous mechanisms aboard *Orzel* were hydraulically operated. The all-welded outer hull was of German-made St52 nickel-chromium steel produced specially for U-boats, of high tensile strength, corrosion-resistant and anti-magnetic. A test depth of 82m (262ft) was easily reached. Drag when submerged was reduced as much as possible, with an obstruction-free deck and a tower of rounded form, with a merged housing for the 105mm (4.1in) deck gun.

Propulsion was from two MAN eight-cylinder diesels of a combined 2386kW (3200hp), and electric motors of 686kW (920hp). Fuel capacity was 136 tonnes (123t). The surface speed of 19.4kt made it one of the faster submarines of the time.

Twelve tubes in all were carried, four each forward, midships (on deck, trainable) and aft. In RN service the AA armament was uprated to a twin Bofors 36mm (1.4in), and a Hotchkiss 13mm (0.5in) heavy machine gun.

A German Atlas-built GHG sonar system was installed.

Orzel

Dimensions: Length 84m (275.6ft), Beam 6.7m (22ft), Draught 4m (13.1ft)

Displacement (surface/submerged): 1117 tonnes (1100t) / 1496 tonnes (1473t)

Propulsion: two diesels of 1193kW (1600hp), two 343kW (460hp) electric motors, two screws

Speed (surface/submerged): 19.4kt (35.9kmh, 22.3mph) / 9kt (16.7kmh, 10.36mph)

Range (surface/submerged): 6230nm (11,538km, 7169mi) / 100nm (185km, 115mi)

Armament: 12 550mm (21.7in) torpedo tubes, 20 torpedoes; one 105mm (4.1in) deck gun; one 13.2mm (0.5in) machine gun

Crew: 60

Orzel

Poland had a five-strong submarine squadron in 1939, three Wilk-class minelayers and two patrol boats. *Orzel*'s sister boat *Sep* escaped to Sweden and was interned. Similar to the Dutch 019 class, they were excellent boats, of welded construction with double hulls and powered by two Sulzer 6QD42 six-cylinder diesels and two Brown-Boveri electric motors.

Leninets class (1931–38)

Germany's declaration of war on the Soviet Union in June 1941 brought about Russia's participation in the Allied war effort on its western fronts (the Soviet Union did not declare war on Japan until August 1945). For the Navy, that meant the Baltic, Barents and Black seas.

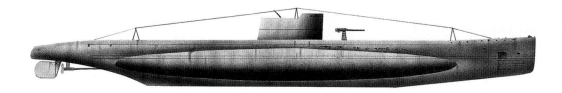

L-3

Submarine war in the Baltic Sea was dominated by extensive minefields and massive nets, often many miles long, set by the Germans and Finns, which the Soviet boats had to skirt. Meanwhile, until the end of 1944, the surface was dominated by German ships. L-3's conning tower has been preserved as a memorial.

The nature of the Baltic and Black seas made the Soviet Navy particularly concerned with mines (Russia's *Krab* of 1912 was the first submarine minelayer), and the large L-class was developed through the 1930s as a minelayer that was also an attack boat. Series I existed only as a draft design. Its prototype was the British L55, sunk in the Baltic in 1919, raised and repaired.

This was a double-hulled design with saddle tanks. These were incorporated into the Russian design, though the L55's auxiliary electric motor, a forerunner of the 'creep motor', was not.

The first three groups, 19 boats in all, had no stern torpedo tubes but carried mines in two stern galleries. In the last two groups to be completed (13 boats) two stern tubes were added. Boats L1 to L6 displayed some problems, including a very slow dive speed, estimated at three minutes, to be corrected in the later builds.

The first group, launched in 1931–32, with three operating in the Black Sea and three in the Baltic, were regarded as underpowered, with diesel engines of 1600kW (2200hp) combined; and electric motors of 1080kW (1450hp). In later L-class groups, the power was doubled.

L-class Series 3

Dimensions: Length 81m (265.75ft), Beam 7.5m (24.6ft), Draught 4.8m (15.75ft)

Displacement (surface/submerged): 1219 tonnes (1200t) / 1573 tonnes (1550t)

Propulsion: two diesels, two electric motors, two screws

Speed (surface/submerged): 15kt (27.8kmh, 17.26mi) / 9kt (16.7kmh, 10.36mph)

Range (surface/submerged): 6000nm (11,112km, 6096 mi) at 9kt / 154nm (285km, 177mi) at 3kt

Armament: five 533mm (21in) torpedo tubes, 12 torpedoes, 20 mines; one 100mm (3.9in), one 45mm (1.75in) gun

Crew: 53

Dekabrist (D-class)

The Soviet Navy's first post-World War I class. Six were built in 1927–29, double-hulled, with electric creep motors and a test depth of 90m (295ft).

Shch class (1932–50)

Eight-eight strong (though 200 were planned), the Shch or *Schuka* ('Pike') was a coastal boat, and as so often is the case, multiple variants appeared even before a new type followed.

Only basic technical details are available of a class that operated from ice-bound to almost subtropical waters, but no doubt there were differences between boats of the same series built at seven yards from Leningrad to Vladivostok. Some were built inland, at Mykolaiv, Ukraine, for example, and sent by river to the Black Sea. Series III's diesel engines were rated at 1021kW (1370hp) and its electric motors at 298kW (400hp), and there seem to have been few basic changes. The towers, however, showed considerable variety,

culminating in the streamlined form of Series X, though its submerged speed of 6.3k t (11.7kmh, 7.2mph) was certainly not special. Operational depth was up to 75m (246ft).

Shch 303

The Baltic was a difficult sea from every point of view. For most of World War II it was a German pond (with Finnish help), with the Soviet fleet hemmed in at Kronstadt and Leningrad, where Submarine Brigades 1 and 2 were based. Only submarines could slip by, and 26 were lost in 1941 alone. It was very late in the war before the Soviet Union gained control.

Schuka **Series X Shch 303**

Dimensions: Length 58.5m (192ft), Beam 6.2m (20.3ft), Draught 4.2m (13.8ft)

Displacement (surface/submerged): 595 tonnes (586t) / 713 tonnes (702t)

Propulsion: two diesels of 510kW (635hp); two 300kW (400hp) electric motors, two screws

Speed (surface/submerged): 12.5kt (23.2kmh, 14.4mph) / 6.3kt (11.7kmh, 7.2mph)

Range (surface/submerged): 6000nm (11,112km, 6905mi) at 8kt / 105nm (194.5km, 121mi) at 2.6kt

Armament: six 553mm (21in) torpedo tubes, 10 torpedoes; two 45mm (1.75in) guns

Crew: 38

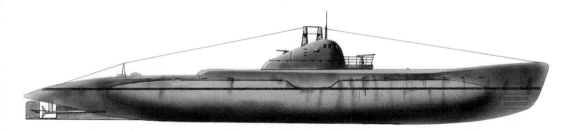

Aerial view of a Soviet S-class submarine. This class of 12 ocean-going boats was built from 1935 into the 1940s. It had four bow and two stern tubes with six reloads. The Soviet Navy classified the first prototypes as IX, with two following versions as IX-bis and IX-bis2. Their nickname of 'Stalinets' was unofficial.

V-boats (1921–34)

Known by V + numeral before they received names in 1931, the nine V-boats played essential parts in the progress towards later classes.

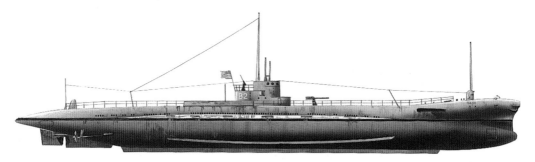

USS *Bass*

Originally V-2, *Bass* was twice the size of the S-boats, with only two more torpedo tubes. It served with Submarine Division 20 in the Caribbean and Pacific. Put on reserve in 1937, recommissioned in 1940, it was part of Submarine Squadron 3, Submarine Division 31, Atlantic Fleet. A fire on 17 August 1942 killed 25 crewmen.

They represented different visions of the future and were not a single class. All presented technical problems, and only the outbreak of war kept them in service. The sequence began in 1921 when V-1, V-2 and V-3 were laid down at Portsmouth Navy Yard. Launched in 1924–28, they were intended as fast fleet submarines.

V-4 (1928), later named *Argonaut* (SM-1), was a minelayer. V-5 and V-6 were submarine cruisers, and V-7, 8 and 9 were general-purpose boats. Comparison of the profiles of USS *Bass* (SS-164) and *Argonaut* shows two very different boats.

V1–3, *Barracuda, Bass, Bonita* (SS-163,164,165) were planned as fast

USS *Bass* (V-1)

Dimensions: Length 104.09m (341.5ft),
Beam 9.4m (27.5ft), Draught 4.62m (15.2ft)

Displacement (surface/submerged): 2153 tonnes
(2119t) / 2546 tonnes (2506t)

Propulsion: two direct drive diesels of 1680kW
(2250hp), two auxiliary 750kW (1000hp) charging diesels; two 890kW (1200hp) electric motors, two screws

Speed (surface/submerged): 21kt (39kmh,
24.2mph) / 9kt (17kmh, 10.3mph)

Range (surface/submerged): 6000nm (11,112km,
6905mi) at 11kt / 90nm (166.7km, 103.6mi) at 5kt

Armament (original): six 533mm (21in) torpedo
tubes, 12 torpedoes; one 127mm (5in) 51cal gun

Crew: 87

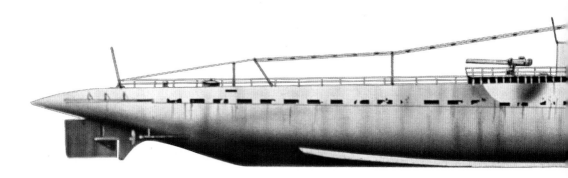

submarines, "not less than 20 knots" to keep with a surface squadron and act as scouts and observers. This required substantial power and fuel reserves. Even so, the required speed was not met, nor was the submerged speed of 9kt; and the Sulzer-Busch engines were unreliable (auxiliary engines replaced 1940, mains 1942–43). Partially double-hulled, they had four forward and two aft 533mm (21in) tubes and carried 12 torpedoes.

USS *Nautilus* (V-6)

Dimensions: Length 113m (371ft), Beam 10.14m (33.3ft), Draught 5.16m (16.9ft)

Displacement (surface/submerged): 2770 tonnes (2730t) / 4000 tonnes (3900t)

Propulsion: two direct drive diesels of 1750kW (2350hp), two auxiliary 300kW (400hp) charging diesels; two 600kW (800hp) electric motors

Speed (surface/submerged): 14kt (26kmh, 16mph) / 6.5kt (12kmh, 7.5mph)

Range (surface/submerged): 9380nm (17,372km, 10,794mi) at 10kt / 90nm (166.7km, 103.6mi) at 5kt

Armament (original): six 533mm (21in) torpedo tubes, 24 torpedoes; two 152mm (6in) 53cal Mk XII Mod2 wet-type deck guns

Crew: 89

The relative size of V-6 is clear as it rests alongside an S-class boat in a fitting-out basin, probably Mare Island.

USS *Nautilus*

The deck guns were designed for the secondary battery of *Lexington*-class battle cruisers and *South Dakota* class battleships, but were only installed in *Omaha*-class cruisers. They fired a 47kg (105lb) shell to a range of 21,310m (69,914ft) at their maximum elevation of 25°.

USS *Dolphin* (V-7)

Dolphin was used through World War II as a
training boat, and was broken up in 1946.

USS *Argonaut* (V-4)

On 1 December 1941, *Argonaut* was stationed off Midway Island on a reconnaissance patrol.
Soon after Pearl Harbor it was converted to a transport and special operations role. In June
1942, along with USS *Nautilus*, it landed 211 US Marines to raid Makin Island, by far the biggest
submarine landing yet attempted.

Welded construction

V-4, *Argonaut* (SM-1) commissioned in
April 1928, was the first US submarine
of partially welded construction,
though riveting was used for the
pressure hull and all vital areas. It
was also the USN's largest until 1958.
Designed as a minelayer, it held 60
mines stored in two galleries and
discharged through 1000mm (40in)
stern chutes. It was also armed with
two forward 533mm (21in) tubes and
two 152mm (6in) guns, forward and
aft of the tower. Unfortunately, its low
speeds limited its value. Re-engined
in 1942, with mine gear removed, and
two external stern tubes fitted, it was
converted to a troop carrier.

V-6, *Nautilus* (SS-168),
commissioned in 1930, was based
on the 'submarine cruiser' concept

– large, well-armed, intended for
long-range patrols. In July 1941, a
refit provided new radio equipment,
two external torpedo tubes at bow
and stern, air conditioning, and new
GM-Winton diesel engines. The
modifications also included internal
rearrangement for conveyance of
special mission troops and supplies.

Air-con

The last V-boat, V-9 *Cuttlefish* (SS-
171) of 1933, was the first submarine
with built-in air conditioning. With
V-8 *Cachalot* (SS-170), it was also
the first to deploy the Mk I Torpedo
Data Computer. With the nine V-boats
completed, the Navy knew what sort
of submarines it wanted and how to
build them. However, it was not wholly
clear on how to use them.

US TORPEDOES

The Mk XIV torpedo, dating from 1931,
was the standard for US submarines
at the start of the war. Despite the
remonstrations of submarine crews,
its serious defects, chiefly in failing
to detonate or under-running the
target, were not fully remedied until
September 1943. With modifications
at last complete, it became a reliable
weapon. Powered by a wet heater
steam turbine with ethanol/methanol
fuel, Model III was 6.25m (20.5ft) long
and weighed 1490kg (3280lb). At 31kt
(57kmh, 35.6mph), it had a range of
8200m (9000yd), which reduced by half
if the speed was set at 45kt (85kmh,
51.8mph). The warhead was 290kg
(643lb) of Torpex.

From 1944, a wakeless, electric-
powered Mk18 torpedo was available,
modelled on the German G7e and widely
used. Of the same dimensions as the
MkXIV, it weighed 1388kg (3061lb),
had a range of 3650m (4000yd) at 29kt
(54kmh, 33.3mph), and a warhead of
270kg (595lb) Torpex or High Blast
explosive.

Salmon class (1936–38)

The USA's oceanic coasts and the remoteness of any likely aggressor ensured that the USN kept a keen interest in developing long-range submarines capable of maintaining surface speed with a battle fleet. This view of the submarines' role was to change in the course of the war.

Salmon (SS-182) was the lead boat of 16, built at Electric Boat, Groton, and the Portsmouth and Mare Island Navy Yards. They were partially double-hulled, and with the preceding P-class, were the first all-welded US submarines. Unusually, air could be pumped into the bow and stern hull spaces to allow access for repairs, even while submerged.

RADAR ON THE FLEET BOATS

One of the first changes made to the older boats during the war was the addition of the SD series air search radar, developed in 1941. The antenna mast, with a 37km (20mi) range, was added to the shears and extended upward from the step perch just aft of the periscopes. In the late spring of 1942, SJ series surface search radar with an 18.5km (10mi) range began to be installed, its normal position on a mast set on the shear beams forward of the periscopes, extending down through the bridge and into the conning tower. By 1944, this was being replaced by SJ-1. Towards the end of the war, the much more effective SV radar with a large wire mesh antenna replaced the SD on the same mast.

Testing

The class was tested to a depth of 76m (250ft). Within the basic configuration, differences between the EB and Navy builds separated *Salmon, Seal* (SS-183) and *Skipjack* (SS-184) from *Snapper, Stingray* and *Sturgeon* (SS-185-187), including tower design (though the 'sail' type of tower was reduced in height on all in the course of the war). On all, the stern was designed to hold two 533mm (21in) torpedo tubes. Four spare torpedoes were initially held in wells in the casing, but this was discontinued in wartime.

Powerplant

The Electric Boat trio were initially powered by four HOV (Hooven-Ovens-Rentschler) nine-cylinder double-action diesels but these proved unsatisfactory in service and after Pearl Harbor were replaced by GM Winton six-cylinder engines. There were two diesel engine rooms plus a motor room. Two engines in the forward engine room drove generators. In the after engine room, two side-by-side engines were joined to reduction gears set forward of the engines, with vibration-isolating hydraulic clutches. The propeller shafts led aft from each of the reduction gears. Two high-speed Elliott-geared electric motors were mounted outboard

USS Salmon

USS *Salmon*, shown here with its pre-war conning tower configuration.

Salmon-class

Dimensions: Length 93.9m (308ft), Beam 7.9m (26.1ft), Draught 4.78m (15.7ft)

Displacement (surface/submerged): 1458 tonnes (1435t) / 2233 tonnes (2198t)

Propulsion (original): four HOR nine-cylinder diesels of 1145kW (1535hp); four 496kW (665hp) geared electric motors, two screws

Speed (surface/submerged): 21kt (39kmh, 24mph) / 9kt (17kmh, 10.3mph)

Range (surface/submerged): 11,000nm (20,372km, 12,659mi) at 10kt / 96nm (178km, 110mi) at 2kt

Armament: eight 533mm (21in) torpedo tubes, 24 torpedoes; one 76mm (3in) 50cal deck gun; four machine guns

Crew: 59

of each shaft, connected directly to the reduction gears.

Surface speed

For surface operation, the engines were clutched to the reduction gears and drove the propellers directly, with the generator engines providing additional voltage to the motors. For submerged operation, the diesels were declutched from the reduction gears and the motors drove the shafts with electricity supplied by the batteries. Fuel capacity was 96,025gal (approx. 355 tonnes), and two 126-cell battery sets supplied submerged power.

Salmon boats carried eight internal torpedo tubes, four bow and four stern, with a warload of 24 torpedoes. A 76mm (3in) 50cal aft-facing deck gun was first installed, later supplemented by four 20mm (0.79in) machine guns. Progressive modifications in detection systems and AA defence were made through the war years.

ENGINE DESIGN, 1930S

One problem shown by the V-boats was the Navy's lack of a reliable diesel engine, especially for large oceanic patrol boats. The answer came from the railways, where compact diesel engines for locomotives had been developed. These were proper diesel-electrics, with the diesel engines acting as electricity generators for high-speed motors that turned the propeller shaft through a reduction-gearing system, which reduced their speed of 1300rpm to a propeller-turning speed of 280rpm. Makers of electric generators and motors included Allis-Chalmers, Westinghouse, Elliott, and General Electric. USS *Porpoise* (SS-172) of 1935 was the first American submarine with diesel-electric transmission, using GM Winton locomotive-type engines. By 1938 (apart from an unhappy flirtation with the HOR engines) US submarines were powered by GM Winton 16-248A or 16-278A engines, or Fairbanks-Morse 38 D8 1/8 engines. Among the advantages of diesel-electric drive was a large reduction in propeller noise as unlike the diesels, the electric motors did not vibrate. Apart from the British V-class, late in the war, the USN was the only navy to use diesel-electric transmission in submarines. All others used direct drive.

USS *Salmon* (SS-182), running speed trials on 29 December 1937.

Gato class (1940–43)

The *Gato* class is the 'fleet submarine' that became a hunter-killer. Following on from two further pre-war classes, Tambor and Gar, the Gato class satisfied the requirements for speed, power, range and armament.

The growing Japanese threat led the US Navy to cling to the concept of the fast fleet submarine even though the speed of battleships and carriers was starting to exceed anything a submarine could manage. When the Pearl Harbor attack changed the nature of a Pacific war from American expectations, they proved successful hunter-killers.

In total, 77 were built, by Electric Boat at Groton, the US Navy yard at Kittery (Maine), Mare Island, and the Manitowoc yard in Wisconsin (finished boats transported in floating drydocks via canals and rivers including the Mississippi to New Orleans). Double-hulled, except for the extremities of the submarine, built of mild steel 12mm (0.56in) thick, and with a welded outer hull, they had an operational depth of 91m (300ft). Internally, they had eight compartments separated by watertight bulkheads. Some of the fuel-holding tanks in the between-space were pressurized. Between the pressure hull and the bridge deck, the conning tower was a horizontal cylinder placed above the control room.

Attack centre

This was the attack centre, with the helm, a chart table, the periscope viewers, radar, sonar and torpedo control. A watertight door opening from it onto the after deck was eliminated from spring 1943. At the aft end of the manoeuvring room was the main control unit with its levers, indicator dials, and switches. The electrically

USS *Gato* (SS-212) off the Mare Island Navy Yard, August 1943.

USS *Ray*

This broadside view shows *Ray* in its original 1943 form. In the course of the war and afterwards, many changes of detail were made in refits.

TDC
Ray was fitted with a Torpedo Data Computer (TDC) linked to the targeting systems, allowing continuous data updates and automatically setting courses right up to the moment of firing. Mark III was the standard, replaced by Mk IV from 1943 on new and refitted boats. As radar became available, it was also linked to the TDC.

Rate of fire
With the ammunition magazine located under the galley and crew's mess aft of the control room, a long passing chain was needed to get shells up to the gun in the forward spot, slowing down firing rates. Eventually, watertight ammunition lockers were placed in the fairwater under the forward gun platform.

Periscope
By the time of *Ray*'s construction, the shears were no longer covered by protective plating, in order to reduce the silhouette.

Look-out platform
The fairwater has been cut away directly under the SD radar mast, leaving a short lip-extension for an aft lookout platform. 'Fairwater' refers to the support structure and plating attached to the main deck and enclosing a free flooding area around the horizontal cylinder of the conning tower, a separate pressure vessel directly above the control room of the submarine. Use of the term 'conning tower' to refer to the combined conning tower and fairwater structure is common but technically inaccurate.

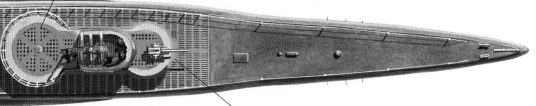

USS *Ray* (SS-271)

Dimensions: Length 95m (311.7ft), Beam 8.31m (27.25ft), Draught 5.2m (17ft)

Displacement (surface/submerged): 1549 tonnes (1525t) / 2463 tonnes (1424t)

Propulsion: four diesel generator engines of a combined 4026kW (5400hp); four 511kW (685hp) geared electric motors, two screws

Speed (surface/submerged): 21kt (39kmh, 24mph) / 9kt (16.6kmh, 10mph)

Range (surface/submerged): 11,000nm (20,372km, 12,659mi) at 10kt / 95nm (176km, 109mi) at 5kt

Armament (original): 10 533mm (21in) torpedo tubes, 24 torpedoes; one 76mm (3in) 50cal deck gun; two 12.7mm (0.5in) machine guns

Crew: 60

Access point
The tower's after end had a watertight access door for the gun crew. This proved to be a liability as several boats had them unseated during depth charge attacks. Moving the gun to the forward position removed the need for the door and in the spring of 1943 it was omitted on *Gatos* under construction, and the concave aft end was changed to an outward-dished convex one.

Deck gun
The deck gun was twice increased in size, first to 101mm (4in) in late 1943, then to 127mm (5in) from late 1944, reflecting the increasing surface activity in destroying small vessels like sampans and trawlers. Fortunately the original specification provided for a gun emplacement robust enough to hold a 127mm (5in) gun.

driven screws were controlled from this station. A watertight bulkhead separated two engine rooms.

Folding bow planes were fitted to control the boat's depth, with fixed stern planes to control its angle in the water. The casing above the pressure hull covered free-flooding space and had a slatted wood walking deck. Retractable mine cable cutters were fitted in the bows of the first 20 boats but removed in 1942 in a drive to eliminate non-essential equipment. A single hydraulically operated rudder was placed between but aft of the two propellers.

Early versions of the class had tall towers (fairwaters in USN parlance) set forward of midships and heightened by a casing around the periscope masts. When SJ radar was installed, its mast was attached aft of the periscopes. The navigation bridge was covered over. Wartime experience saw these features gradually cut back and the fairwater extended lengthwise with gun platforms (most of the class went through three makeovers). Aft of the shears was a lower open deck above the housing for the main induction valve. To the crew, it was the cigarette deck, but most of it was soon taken up by a 40mm (1.5in) AA gun.

Different finishing touches were put depending on whether the builders were private or government

CAMOUFLAGE

Until 1944, US submarines' basic wartime paint was black, classified as Ms (Measure) 9, and considered the most effective method of concealment. Some submarines in the Pacific had the lower hulls painted dark blue, but this proved to turn pale too quickly. Ms 10, introduced in June 1942, specified 'Ocean Grey' for best concealment from surface vessels. From early 1944, a combination of black with shades of grey was also used, going stem-to-stern from Haze Grey to Mid-Grey, then black, in styles Ms 32/9SS (known as the dark grey job) and Ms 32 3/SS-B (the light grey job). Decks were gloss black and the undersides of gun platforms were countershaded in white. Boats carried different camouflage patterns at different times. Individual variations were few: the commander of *Gato*-class USS *Harder* (SS-257), aware of the Purkinje visual effect, added a touch of red to Ms 32 3/SS-B, making a pink effect.

(Portsmouth always set the anchor on the port bow and cut 'limber holes' in the casing above the pressure hull, while EB cut a long slit on each side and sited the anchor to starboard). Two small boats (later only one) were held under deck hatches, and escape hatches were fitted above the forward and aft torpedo rooms. Two rescue buoys on cables were stowed under the deck, and connection points were fitted to allow air to be pumped in in the case of rescue or salvage.

Bespoke upgrades

From September 1942, the plating around the periscopes was removed on

almost all *Gatos*, and around the same time, the plating bulwark around the aft section of the fairing was removed and replaced by railings, giving the boats a quite different look. Many other detail changes, often done 'bespoke' for individual boats, were made as well, with additional ammunition lockers, ladders down from the cigarette deck, rearranged lookout perches, and spindle mounts for .50cal machine guns. A Torpedo Director Transmitter was mounted aft of the SD radar mast to pass down instructions for surface firing, and a 228.6mm (9in) searchlight for night action was fitted on a swinging bracket. The venturi, or wind-deflector,

USS *Drum* (SS-228)

The first *Gato* boat to be commissioned and enter combat, *Drum* is seen here in World War II mode. After suffering heavy depth-charging it was given a *Balao*-type conning tower at the end of 1943. The complex rig above the shears reflects the variety of sensory and communications equipment.

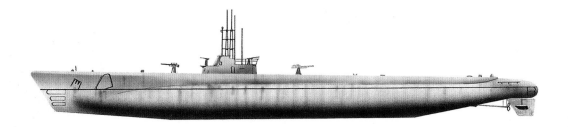

USS *Grouper* (SS-214)

Commissioned on 12 February 1942, *Grouper* made nine war patrols, and in 1946 was the first submarine fitted with a combat information centre. From then on it was a test boat, becoming the first designated SSK on 2 January 1951. Later a floating laboratory, AGSS-214, it was finally scrapped in 1970.

USS *Barb* (SS-220)

Barb made five patrols off Europe before deploying to Pearl Harbor in September 1943. On seven Pacific patrols it sank 17 ships of 96,628GRT, including the escort carrier *Unyo* on 17 September 1944, making it the US Navy's most successful combat submarine. Members of its crew mounted the only land incursion into Japan, in July 1945.

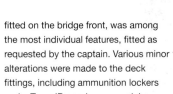

fitted on the bridge front, was among the most individual features, fitted as requested by the captain. Various minor alterations were made to the deck fittings, including ammunition lockers and a Type JP passive sonar globe mounting, to supplement the keel-fitted Type FM sonar array.

A *Gato* class boat could stay submerged for up to 48 hours, but such a length was rare. Crew accommodation included showers, refrigerated food, ice, mess room above the battery compartment, seating 24, clothes washers, and bunks. Air conditioning was installed, both in the interest of crew comfort and to reduce the risk of fires caused by condensation water in the increasingly complex electrical installations.

All Gatos had diesel-electric drive with four diesel engines generating

power for four water-cooled 1300rpm electric motors which turned the shafts via reduction gears. Twelve built by Electric Boat had HOR double-acting diesel engines, later replaced by either General Motors Cleveland 16/278A V-type or Fairbanks-Morse 38D 81/8 nine-cylinder opposed-piston engines, both types being two-stroke. The electric motors were from the Elliott and General Electric companies, the former normally paired with F-M engines and the latter with the GM engines. Two Sargo battery sets each had 126 cells, with a total weight of 208 tonnes (204.6t). Fuel capacity, originally 94,000 gals (approx. 348 tonnes) was increased to 116,000 gals (approx. 429 tonnes) by using some of the ballast tanks.

The motors and generators were built by General Electric,

Westinghouse, Allis-Chalmers, and Elliot. Westinghouse GE and Cutler-Hammer also built the main control units (switchboards). Installation of a GE switchboard usually meant the boat would also have GE motors and generators. Westinghouse controls were used with their own motors and generators, or with the Elliott machinery. Cutler-Hammer controls were generally linked with Allis-Chalmers motors and generators.

Auxiliary motors

Apart from the main drive systems, around 40 auxiliary motors of various capacities provided for the operation of compressors, blowers, pumps, hydraulic accumulators, pneumatic systems and other equipment. Electric current for operation of these motors was supplied by the auxiliary generator, the main batteries, or a combination of both, through two auxiliary distribution switchboards. The forward distribution switchboard, connected to the forward battery, fed all auxiliary machines in and forward of the control room, while the after-distribution switchboard, powered by the after battery or the auxiliary generator, fed all auxiliary machines aft of the control room. A bus-tie circuit connected the two switchboards, making it possible to feed one switchboard from the other in the event of an emergency.

Modifications

While the basic specification hardly changed, six different modifications were applied to the class (not all of them to all boats) with the aim of reducing the profile and extending space for gun mountings, antennas and observation platforms.

Model 1: original specification
Model 1A: shortened pilot house forward of the bridge
Model 2A (September 1942): shear plating removed
Model 3 (late 1942): fairing removed from around pilot house, ammunition locker placed under forward gun platform, additional AA gun installed
Model 3A: SJ radar mast moved from bridge to aft of shears
Model 4: bridge deck lowered; plating removed from around the shear support beams (the 'covered wagon' look)

Weaponry

The *Gatos* had the standard fleet boat set of six forward and four aft 533mm (21in) torpedo tubes. Mines could be substituted for torpedoes, one torpedo being replaced by two Mk 10 or Mk 12 mines, giving a maximum capacity of 48 mines. However, standard practice

was to retain at least four torpedoes on minelaying missions, reducing mine load to 40.

Artillery on board varied in type and location. The original fitting was a single 76mm (3in) 50cal deck gun, and a 50cal wet (water-cooled) M2 machine gun placed aft of the bridge. Later, in 1942, this was replaced by a 20mm (0.79in) AA gun on a tripod mount. Another was installed in front of the cut-back fairwater. From 1943, most boats acquired a 102mm (4in) 50cal deck gun, usually placed on the after deck. Final arrangements were a 127mm (5in) 25cal aft-sited deck gun (first deployed on USS *Spadefish* (SS-411) in May 1944); a 40mm (1.5in) AA gun below the bridge, and a 20mm (0.79in) AA gun on the foredeck; or 40mm AA on the

fairwater platforms and a twin 20mm (0.79in) AA on the foredeck, along with the more powerful aft deck gun.

Spindles were fitted on the bridge and fairwater sides for portable machine guns. The proliferation of guns was partly through the danger of *kamikaze* attacks, but also many small merchant and military vessels were attacked on the surface without the use of torpedoes.

Perhaps the main minus point of these all-round capable submarines, indeed of all the fleet boats, was a rather ponderous manoeuvrability, a result of their large size. Some rudder experiments were tried without success. But dive time, which had been slow in previous classes, was down to 30–35 seconds by 1943.

USS *Greenling* (SS-213) shows off her 127mm (5in) and 40mm (1.57in) deck guns while moored in Mare Island Navy Yard, California, 8 May 1945.

Balao class (1942–44)

The *Balao* was the largest class of submarine in the US Navy.

The USN was aware that Japanese depth charges were effective to 90m (295ft) and that the *Gato* class's operating depth was down to only 91.4m (300ft). Greater depth ability was needed. By changing the pressure hull cover to High Tensile Steel (HTS) 20mm (0.79in) thick, a maximum diving depth of 198m (650ft) could be achieved. In the interest of safety, the test depth of the *Balao* design was finally fixed at 123m (400ft).

The *Gato* plans were modified to incorporate the thicker pressure hull. The design was otherwise so similar to the later *Gatos*, apart from accessories and minor details, that USS *Balao* (SS-285) and others of its class were being laid down even as the last of the *Gato* boats were nearing completion.

From the start, the Balaos had a very much cut-down fairwater, so much so that the gun platforms had to be extended over the deck. The two tapering and robust periscopes were the main visual definer between the 121 *Balaos* and the *Gatos*, the latter with thinner scopes and supporting ribs. Supporting brackets were mounted two-thirds of the way up and at the top of the shears and were extended back to the SJ surface radar mast and the base part of the telescopic air search

On patrol in the Pacific, USS *Batfish* slices through the water at high speed to intercept a target detected on their SJ (surface search) radar.

SD mast. Both of these masts were braced to the shears with flat horizontal stiffening brackets. Just aft of the SD mast was the pedestal for the Target Bearing Transmitter.

Fitted between the shear tubes was the loop antenna of the LF radio receiver. The small stub antennas

USS *Entemedor* (SS-340)

Entemedor returned to base at Seattle on 22 September 1945, and served with the Pacific Fleet at Subic Bay in 1946–47. In reserve between 1948 and 1950, it was recommissioned in October 1950, joined the Atlantic Fleet, went through a GUPPY IIA refit in 1952, and did stints with the 6th Fleet in the Mediterranean up to 1962.

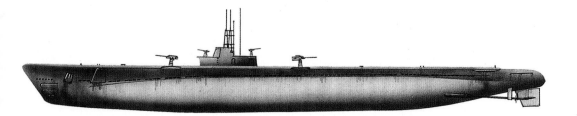

on the forward edge of the number one periscope shear were the first installations of radar countermeasures gear, installed on USS *Balao* in 1944. The APR stub at the top could detect low-frequency signals and the AS-44 antenna below it was used for microwave (S-band) detection. They had no jamming capabilities and were only for detection and classification. *Balao* was also refitted with a new No. 1 periscope which supplemented the optics with a small range-only radar transmitter/receiver built into the head. This ST radar eliminated the guesswork involved in getting an accurate range to a target while making a submerged approach

Many boats had a rotating T-shaped bar on the foredeck, the head of a JT passive sonar supplementing the standard retractable QB/QC transducers

mounted forward on the keel. As with the *Gatos*, design features varied according to the builder. A reduction in the size of the main induction valve allowed for a tapered end of the fairwater in the Navy design, with more deck room, but this was replaced by a more usable rounded end. A useful feature of all the class was a watertight trunk from the deck to the control room, allowing gun crews to reach position without going through the packed conning tower. Another typical feature was the 'bullnose' hole in the bow, for towing or mooring attachment.

Propulsion was as for the Gato class, with the same tankage and battery capacity.

In 1943–44 Electric Boat and then Manitowoc reversed the placing of the radar masts, with the SJ moved forward

of the SD, and then made a further change in spring 1944, with 20 boats having a redesigned mast, similar to the periscopes, for the wider Type SV radar antenna, and the LF antenna placed between this and the aft periscope shear. The majority of these boats were commissioned too late for active war service. Older boats, including USS *Balao*, from mid-1944, had their SD mast moved further aft, and rebuilt in the style of the SV mast. By 1944 new electronic countermeasures equipment was being installed, with stub antennas attached to the forward periscope shear, APR for detecting low-frequency signals and AS-44 for microwave (S-band). From November 1944, the Kollmorgen Type 4 periscope, with the new ST firing range radar, to augment the on-board SJ radar, was operational

Radar mast
The shears arrangement has been reduced and simplified compared with the *Gato* boats. Aft of the scope tubes are the SJ surface search radar mast and the extendable SD air search radar mast. Alterations of this positioning were constant among the class.

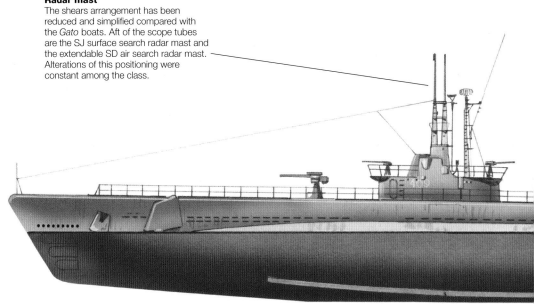

on the *Balao*-class *Spikefish* (SS 404).
This was also the first to be fitted with
hydraulic periscope hoists replacing the
cable and motor arrangement. Not all
boats received these novel items.

Guns on the early *Balao* class were
a forward-mounted 100mm (4in) 50cal
Mk 9 deck gun, and a single 20mm
(0.79in) Oerlikon automatic cannon
on tripod mounts on the fairwater's
gun decks. As the class increased,
armament became heavier and more
varied. Later or refitted boats had a
127mm (5in) 25cal Mk 17 deck gun,
either forward, aft, or both; a Bofors
40mm (1.5in) Mk3 on both platforms;
and a 20mm (0.79in) Mk 10 aft, in
addition to machine gun positions as
on the *Gatos*. USS *Blower* and others,
with the main gun aft, had an additional
20mm (0.79in) Mk10 mount on the

foredeck. A circular ready service
ammunition locker was installed below
the forward gun deck.

USS *Piper* (SS-409)

Dimensions: Length 95m (311.7ft), Beam 8.3m
(27.25ft), Draught 5.1m (16.8ft)

Displacement (surface/submerged): 1550 tonnes
(1526t) / 2440 tonnes (2401t)

Propulsion: four F-M diesel generator engines of
a combined 4026kW (5400hp); two 511kW (685hp)
Elliott geared electric motors, two screws

Speed (surface/submerged): 21kt (39kmh, 24mph)
/ 9kt (16.6kmh, 10mph)

Range (surface/submerged): 11,000nm (20,372km,
12,659mi) at 10kt / 95nm (176 km, 109mi) at 5kt

Armament: 10 533mm (21in) torpedo tubes, 24
torpedoes; one 127mm (5in) 25cal deck gun, one
40mm (1.5in) Bofors, one twin 20mm (0.79in) Oerlikon
AA gun

Crew: 80

USS *Piper* (SS-409)

Though American fleet submarines did serve as
fleet escorts and scouts, especially to carrier
groups, they also had a 'hunter-killer' role in
seeking out and destroying Japanese naval craft.
Smaller vessels were usually sunk by gunfire.

Armament
Some *Balao* class submarines
acquired a second Mk 17
127mm (5in) deck gun from late
1943, as torpedo-worthy targets
were becoming scarce.

Power supply
All *Balao* submarines were diesel-electric
with engines from Fairbanks-Morse or
General Motors. Piper was driven by four
Fairbanks-Morse Model 38D8-1/8
10-cylinder opposed diesel engines
driving electric generators that powered
two low-speed Elliott electric motors.

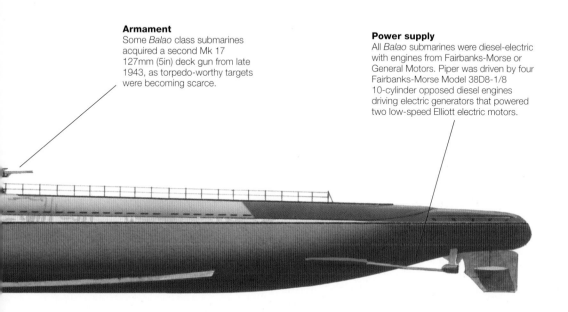

Tench class (1944–45)

The US Navy's final submarine class of the war, the type served in modernized form for another 30 years.

Ten *Tench*-class were completed in time for war service. They were almost identical in externals to the Balao boats, though the fairwater was even shorter, and the overhang of the aft gun platform often had a supporting stanchion.

The arrangement of limber holes in the outer hull depended on the building design. Electric Boat (EB) went for a row of half-moon shapes along each side while the Navy design used oval holes in a double row forward and a single row aft. The open deck was laid with teak slats, almost to the bow with EB boats and only a short section fore and aft of the fairwater on the Navy boats. Rearrangement of the folded bow planes from parallel to the deck, as built, was frequent, with the rigging mechanism altered to set them at an angle so that they would guide the boat down faster when rigged out.

Internally there were significant differences based on experience in action. The tankage arrangement was completely redesigned with all the piping. This eliminated vent riser pipes

passing through the forward torpedo room from main ballast tank No.1. The tank was full when submerged and depth charge damage to the vent pipes would have flooded the torpedo room. There were only three main ballast tanks (1, 2, & 6) and two fuel ballast tanks (3 & 5). No.7 main ballast tank was dispensed with and used as a supplementary fuel tank. Total fuel capacity was 113,000 gals (427,140l). A redesign of the torpedo rooms allowed for four extra torpedoes: 28 in all. Adjacent to the control room was a large magazine holding 1300 rounds for the 40mm, and 120 rounds for the

FIRE CONTROL

US submarines had the best fire control system of the war, the Torpedo Data Computer (TDC), developed by the Arma company. An early electromechanical analogue computer, it not merely provided the best immediate firing solution, but fed information into the torpedo which enabled it to track the moving target. Located in the conning tower, it was a bulky device requiring a technician and an operator, but its precision outclassed German, Japanese and British fire control devices. In Mk I form, it was retrofitted into pre-war boats; submarines from the *Tambor* class (1940) onwards were designed to hold the Mk III version.

USS *Tench* (SS-417)

Dimensions: Length 95m (311.7ft), Beam 8.33m (27.3ft), Draught 5.18m (17ft)

Displacement (surface/submerged): 1800 tonnes (1750t) / 2455 tonnes (2416t)

Propulsion: four diesel generator engines of a combined 4026kW (5400hp); four 511kW (685hp) electric motors, two screws

Speed (surface/submerged): 21kt (39kmh, 24mph) / 9kt (16.6kmh, 10mph)

Range (surface/submerged): 11,000nm (20,372km, 12,659mi) at 10kt / 95nm (176km, 109mi) at 5kt

Armament: 10 533mm (21in) torpedo tubes, 28 torpedoes; one 127mm (5in) deck gun, one Bofors 40mm (1.5in), one twin Oerlikon 20mm (0.79in) AA gun

Crew: 81

USS *Pickerel* (SS-524)

Pickerel was launched on 8 February 1944. In 1949, it deployed to Submarine Division II at Pearl Harbor, and thereafter remained in the Pacific. In 1962, it received a GUPPY III refit, then joined the 7th Fleet at Yokosuka, Japan. After Vietnam combat deployment on Yankee Station, it was transferred to Italy in 1972 as *Primo Longobardo*.

127mm (5in) guns. Further pressure-proof ammunition stowage tubes were set at deck level close to the guns forward and aft of the fairwater.

From stem to stern, the compartments consisted of a forward torpedo room with escape trunk; officers' quarters (above the forward battery); control room, with pump room, stores, and access hatch to conning tower above; crew's mess and crew's quarters, with aft battery below; forward engine room; aft engine room; machine room with manoeuvring room above; aft torpedo room. Crew accommodation was the best of all wartime submarines.

Diesel-electric propulsion in previous classes had involved two or four electric motors coupled to the propeller shafts through reduction gearboxes. These were complex, easily damaged and hard to repair. Though quieter than direct drive, they still made some underwater noise. By early 1944, a low-speed double armature motor had been developed by Navy engineers, capable of driving a shaft on its own without gearing. The first set was installed on USS *Sea Owl* (SS-405). Built by Elliott, General Electric, and Westinghouse, these large motors, developing 2500kW (3352hp), proved both quieter and more shock-resistant than the reduction gearing.

Armament

As designed, the *Tench* boats carried a single 127mm (5in) 25cal gun aft of the tower, and two 40mm (1.5in) AA guns on the fairwater platforms. Spindle mounts for portable 50cal machine guns were mounted on the bridge and alongside the fairwater. Some boats including USS *Thornback* (SS-418) had an additional twin 20mm (0.79in) mounting on the foredeck.

Even in their brief wartime careers, individual boats underwent some modification. USS *Tirante* (SS-420) had a second 40mm (1.5in) gun installed at Pearl Harbor, and its forward escape trunk was rigged as a 'foxhole' to hold a .50 cal machine gun with the operator standing in the hatch. More topside pressure-proof stowages were added. Its armament then comprised one 127mm (5in)/25cal gun facing aft, two 40mm (1.5in) Bofors guns on the fairwater gun platforms, one forward, one aft; one 20mm (0.79in) Oerlikon and two .50cal machine guns on foredeck; one .50cal in foxhole; plus spindle mounts for additional machine guns.

This reflects the late stage of the Pacific war, with operations chiefly on the surface against small vessels, and strong AA defence required.

Two US submariners enjoy a break of patrol at Dutch Harbor in the Aleutian Islands.

USS *Tench* (SS-417)

The *Tench* class had a low superstructure and hull profile, and streamlined lines that gave it a good surface speed.

LF loop antenna
This was mounted between the periscopes, although later *Tench*-class boats had it mounted on a bracket aft of the SJ mast.

Ballast tanks
Re-planning of the ballast tanks also allowed space for an additional four torpedoes compared with the *Balao* and *Gato* boats.

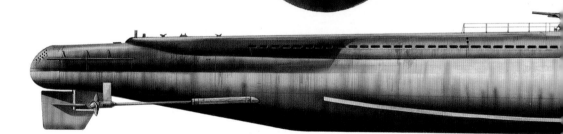

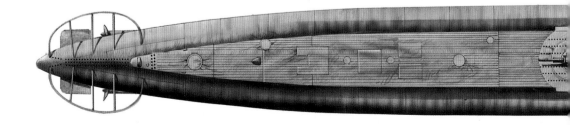

Battery
Two 126-cell Sargo batteries were carried in forward and after compartments. Designed by the Bureau of Steam Engineering, they were named for USS *Sargo* whose commissioning C.O., Lieutenant E. E. Yeomans, suggested the design. Cells had two concentric hard rubber cases with a layer of soft rubber between them. This helped to prevent leakage of sulphuric acid in the event of depth charging or ramming.

Dive planes
Forward diving planes were stowed ready-tilted in dive position so that when extended they would immediately force the bow down. Diving to periscope depth could be achieved in 30–40 seconds.

1ST FLOTILLA INSIGNIA

Many U-boats had insignia (*Bootswappen*) painted on their conning towers. The first examples were individual, but later boats often carried a flotilla insignia as well.

2ND FLOTILLA INSIGNIA

The 2nd Flotilla insignia consisted of a U-boat transfixed by a shaft of lightning, otherwise known as the *Siegesrune*. This symbol was a runic depiction of the letter 'S', standing for *Sieg*, or victory.

3RD FLOTILLA INSIGNIA

Fewer 3rd Flotilla boats carried the unit badge – the turtle – than was common in other units, which may be why it is not as well known as the Bull of the 7th Flotilla or the Laughing Swordfish of the 9th Flotilla.

4TH FLOTILLA INSIGNIA

The 4th Flotilla had no recorded flotilla insignia other than standard training markings. Some boats acquired individual insignia: that carried by U-3030 was designed by the first officer Oblt. Dr Hansmann.

5TH FLOTILLA INSIGNIA

U-boat insignia varied from the overtly military through humorous to personal emblems of the commander. Many had an underwater theme, the rarely seen 5th Flotilla's insignia being a seahorse.

6TH FLOTILLA INSIGNIA

Originally carried by Otto von Bülow's U-404, the 6th Flotilla emblem was a U-boat silhouette over a stylized Viking ship prow. It may have also been used by the 23rd Flotilla under von Bülow's command.

7TH FLOTILLA INSIGNIA

The 'Snorting Bull' was originally the emblem of U-47, after Gunther Prien's nickname of 'the Bull'. Designed by Engelbert Endrass, it was later selected as the 7th Flotilla's insignia.

8TH FLOTILLA INSIGNIA

U-boat insignia derived from a number of different sources. The 8th Flotilla was founded at Königsberg, but moved to Danzig in 1942, and the flotilla symbol incorporated the latter city's coat of arms.

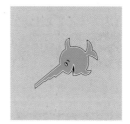

9TH FLOTILLA INSIGNIA

The 9th Flotilla's 'Laughing Swordfish' was famous. Originally the emblem of Heinrich Lehmann-Willenbrock's U-96, it became the flotilla's insignia when the ace commander took over the unit.

10TH FLOTILLA INSIGNIA

Overtly nationalistic or Nazi symbols were rare on U-boat insignia during World War II. The 10th Flotilla was the only unit that carried the *Balkenkreuz* more usually seen on aircraft or military vehicles.

11TH FLOTILLA INSIGNIA
Given that the 11th Flotilla's main operational area was in the Arctic, it is not surprising that the unit's insignia should depict a polar bear riding on the back of a surfaced U-boat.

12TH FLOTILLA INSIGNIA
The insignia of a wolf's head over a U-boat silhouette was mounted over a globe showing Eurasia, all within a black 'U' for U-boat. Few 12th Flotilla boats actually carried the unit insignia.

13TH FLOTILLA INSIGNIA
The Viking ship on a white cross was an appropriate symbol for a unit based in Norway. About 10 of the flotilla's boats have been recorded as carrying the flotilla insignia.

19TH FLOTILLA INSIGNIA
Although the 19th Flotilla had its own insignia of a stag's head, the four Type IIC boats assigned to the unit carried their own symbols, originally applied while they had been front boats with the 1st Flotilla.

23RD FLOTILLA INSIGNIA
Most of the boats assigned to the 23rd Flotilla wore individual insignia. Indications are that the 'White Donkey', thought to be the flotilla's device, was carried only by Hans Heidtmann's U-559.

24TH FLOTILLA INSIGNIA
There is scant evidence to suggest that any of the 24th Flotilla's boats used the official emblem, the stag's antler insignia. At least eight boats carried a white 'V' on the side of the conning tower.

26TH FLOTILLA INSIGNIA
Unlike the 25th Flotilla, the 26th Flotilla did have boats permanently assigned, and there is no record that any of them carried the unit's official insignia. Most were former combat boats with their own symbols.

29TH FLOTILLA INSIGNIA
The flotilla's insignia was originally worn by U-338. The boat rammed a dock crane on being launched, and became known as the 'Wild Donkey'.

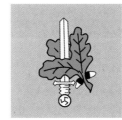

U-857 INSIGNIA
There is no photographic evidence that the 33rd Flotilla had a unit insignia. However, many of the boats used their own symbols, like the sword and oak leaves carried by the Type IXC/40 boat U-857.

Index

Note: page numbers in
bold refer to images or
information contained in
captions.

'600' and '630' classes
    France 78, **78–9, 79**
    Italy 47

A

accommodation 39, 84,
    113,119
acoustic protection 33,
    64,**68**,98
Adua **48–9**
Aichi M6A Seiran 65, **67**
air conditioning 39, 77,
    106,113
aircraft
    France **82, 83**
    German rotary kites **31**
    Japan 60, 65, **65, 67**
Ammiraglio Cagni 52, **52**
anchor chains **23**
Angelo Emo **50**
antennas 115–16, **120**
    see also radar
anti-vibration wires **23**
Antonio Sciesa 44
Argonaut, USS (V-4)
    106,**106**
Argonaute 78, **78–9**
Ariane **7**
armaments *see* guns and
    mountings; torpedoes
asbestos 98
ASDIC (sonar) 87, 95, 97

B

back-up controls **38**
Balao, USS (SS-285) 115,
    116
ballast tanks 118, **120**

Baltic Sea 102, **102–3**
Barb, USS (SS-220) **113**
Barbarigo 50, **50**
Bass, USS (V-1) 104–5, **104**
Batfish, USS **115**
batteries
    Germany 19, 37
    Italy 37
    Japan 68
    United Kingdom 84, 88,
        90, 94
    United States 113, **121**
Besson MB-41-0 floatplane
    82, **83**
Black Sea 102
Blower, USS 117
bow planes *see* dive planes

C

Cachalot, USS (V-8) 106
Calosi, Carlo 49
camouflage **20–1**, 100, 112
Casabianca **76**, 77
colour schemes **83**, 100
    see also camouflage
crew accommodation
    see accommodation
Cuttlefish, USS (V-9) 106

D

Dagabur 49, **49**
Delfino 46, **46**
detection systems *see* radar;
    sonar
diesel-electric transmission
    89, 96, 108, 113, **117**
direct drive 19, 89
dive planes
    Germany 18, **21**
    Japan 68, **68**
    United Kingdom 91
    United States 112, 118,
        121

diving depth *see* operating
    depth
Dolphin, USS (V-7) **106**
Domenico Millelire **45**
double hulls
    France 76, **76**, 78, **80**, 81
    Germany 12, 29, 34
    Italy 42, 44, **45**, 56
    Japan 60, 62, 71
    Poland **101**
    Soviet Union 102, **102**
    United Kingdom 88,
        89
    United States 105, 107
    see also pressure hulls
drive systems
    diesel-electric
        transmission 89, 108,
        113, **117**, 119
    direct drive 19, 89
Drum, USS (SS-228) **112**

E

endurance period *see* patrol
    length
engine design 108
Enrico Tazzoli 45, **45**
Enrico Toti 44, **45**
Entemedor, USS (SS-340)
    115
escape systems 95
escape trunks 119
Espadon **80**

F

fairwaters **111**, 112
Filippo Corridoni **43**
fire control 38, 118
flak platforms **26**, 27
Flutto 57, **57**
Focke-Achgelis (Fa-330)
    30, 31, **31**
France 74, 76–83

'600' and '630' classes
    (1927–45) 78
    Argonaute 78, **78–9**
    Ariane 79
'1500' Type (1924–43)
    76–7
    Casabianca **76**, 77
    Henri Poincaré **76**
    Rubis 77
    Sfax 77
Requin class
    Espadon **80**
    Requin **80**
Sirène class, *Galathée*
    80
Surcouf (1929) 81–2,
    81–3

G

Galatea 47, **47**
Galathée **80**
Gato, USS (SS-212) **109**
Germany 6, 9, 12–41
    Type IA (1936–40) 12
    U-25 12, **12**
    Type II (1935–41) **19**
    Type IIA 13, **13**, 14
    U-2 13, **13**
    U-4 **14**
    U-6 **14**
    Type IIB 13, **14**
    Type IIC 15, **15**
    Type IID 15, **15**
    U-137 15
    Type VII (1935–45) **8–9**,
        17, 37
    Type VIIA (U-27 to
        U-36) 17–19
    U-32 17, **17**
    Type VIIB 19, 22, **26, 33**
    U-47 **6**, **20–1**, **24**
    U-84 **26**
    U-99 **19**

Picture Credits

AirSeaLand Images: 6, 7, 14, 17, 19, 23, 24, 28, 35, 37, 62, 65, 72, 77, 79, 83, 87, 91, 97, 99, 100, 103, 115, 119

Alamy: 44, 46, 50

Amber Books: 8, 16, 18, 33, 81

Getty Images: 42, 53, 94

Naval History & Heritage Command: 11, 15, 54, 55, 58, 59, 63, 69, 70, 75, 105, 108, 109, 114

ARTWORK CREDITS:
All artworks copyright Amber Books Ltd, except page 31 courtesy Vincent Bourguignon and pages 68–69, 78–79, 84–85 and 89 courtesy Pavel Matviyenko.